WALKING IN THE

Walking in the Clouds

Impressions of Nepal

Judy Lomax

ROBERT HALE · LONDON

First published in Great Britain 1981

ISBN 0 7091 8831 5

Robert Hale Ltd
Clerkenwell House
Clerkenwell Green
London EC1R 0HT

Photoset by Specialised Offset Services Limited, Liverpool
and printed in Great Britain by
Lowe & Brydone Ltd, Thetford, Norfolk
Bound by Weatherby Woolnough, Northants.

Contents

Illustrations

Between pages 144 and 145

Maps

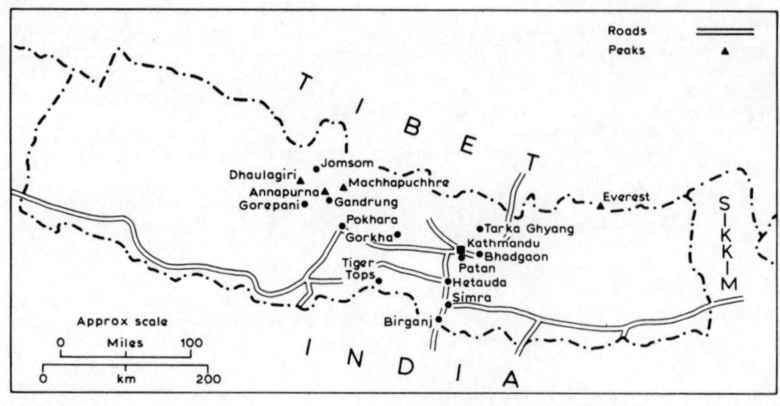

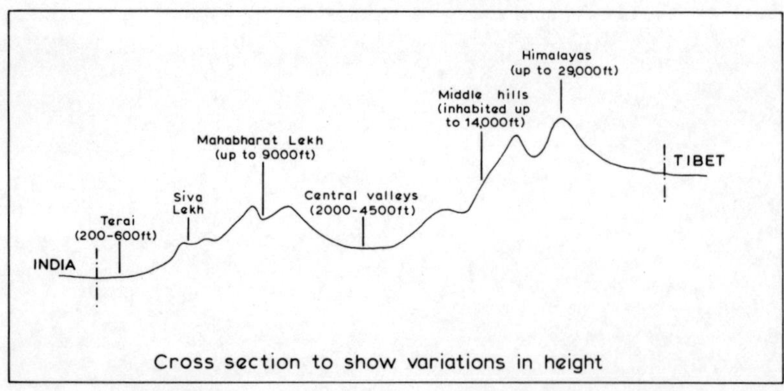

Nepal, showing long-distance roads and main places mentioned in the text.

Introduction

At last, nearly three years after the death of the Hindu Shah King Mahendra of Nepal, the Nepalese court astrologers had agreed on the most propitious date for the coronation of his son, Birendra Bir Bikram Shah Dev, the only Hindu monarch in the world.

At home, in Berkshire, we had been waiting impatiently for their decision, as my husband David, a BBC television reporter, had been assigned to a documentary film about the coronation and we had decided to cash all our savings so that I and our three children could go with him. We had been invited to stay in Kathmandu with Nepalese friends, Jaya and Kanti Giri, both doctors, whom we had known for many years, and with a school friend, David Waterhouse, who was in Nepal with his family for the British Council.

Until as recently as 1950, our visit would have been impossible, as Nepal was closed to foreigners. Only a handful of privileged western diplomats and explorers had ever visited its capital, Kathmandu, and even fewer had been allowed into the interior. This isolation was the deliberate policy of the Ranas, who had ruled the country for a century as autocratic hereditary prime ministers, and before them of the Shah kings who had united the country in the eighteenth century. In 1950, the Shah king Tribhuvan, Birendra's grandfather, regained control of the country and opened its borders.

Nepal's geography had helped to keep outsiders out, and still, in spite of its exotic attraction, makes communications within the country difficult. The Himalayas, popularly believed to be the home of innumerable gods, tower along the northern border, and until recently the Terai, which merges only a few hundred feet above sea level with the Indian plains, formed an equally inhospitable barrier of malarial swamp and jungle.

The people of Nepal are a mixture of races, with a corresponding variety of traditions. Several dozen distinct tribal groups, each with its own customs, live in the valleys and on the lower slopes of the Himalayas, in the central valley of Kathmandu and its towns, and in the tropical Terai. The majority still lead a tough life of poverty and self-sufficiency, supported by a rich combination of Hindu and Buddhist beliefs. As Nepal has escaped western colonization, it is one of the few countries in the world where the culture has survived without the distortion of outside influences, although these are inevitably felt now that Kathmandu is linked to the outside world both by air and by a few long-distance roads.

We left England on a raw January evening in the mid 1970s. Jane, Alistair, and Megan, who were eleven, ten, and five, had even less idea than I had of what to expect. I had read everything I could find about Nepal, but soon realized that this had given me a confused and even at times misleading idea of the country. Although it is roughly the same size as England, it is still only possible to visit most of the country on foot, and Nepal has such a wide variety of scenery, climate, culture and tradition that it is impossible to include them all in one book – or indeed to know them all. I have tried, through our own experiences and observations, to give a general impression of what life in Nepal is like, and why, and hope that this has captured something of its spirit.

1

First Impressions: Kathmandu

The Himalayas were like sharp white clouds crystallized in the distance against a clear blue sky as we flew over the northern plains of India. Below us on the right snaked the sacred River Ganges and ahead, on the left, Annapurna and Dhaulagiri were easily identifiable. As the plane turned steeply the pilot told us that Everest was visible on the right, but we could not distinguish it from the other mountains in the long jagged line separating Nepal from Tibet.

The approach to Kathmandu was over rugged flat-topped hills with what looked from the air like strange geological contours, the outlines of terraced paddy fields rising tier upon tier. Less than an hour after leaving Delhi we had already crossed the Nepalese Terai, the low lying flat southern area which merges only a few hundred feet above sea level into the Indian plains, and the Mahabharat Mountains which form a 9,000-foot barrier to the south of the Kathmandu valley.

Kathmandu airport seemed small and provincial after the bustle of Delhi. A minibus took us the three miles into the city centre, along a wide pot-holed road lined by circular painted brick tree-protectors, like giant incinerators, each one surrounding a newly planted sapling, to a hotel at the junction of old and new Kathmandu. A straight mile of more or less modern shops known as New Road ended at crossroads in the middle of which stood a statue of King Tribhuvan, father of modern Nepal, on a raised pedestal; the other three streets led into a maze of old city bazaars and temples.

We spent our first day in Kathmandu wandering around, soaking up the atmosphere, allowing ourselves to be overwhelmed by sight, sound and smell. There are said to be 30,000 people living in every square mile of the city, in tall narrow houses terraced round inner courtyards and along tiny alleyways, and most of them seemed to be in the bazaar. As obvious newcomers we were immediately surrounded by boys trying to sell us postcards, bangles, model Buddhas, all at "very cheap price – very good quality". One, more persistent than the rest, to whom we explained that "Today we are just looking; we will buy another day", followed us for some time, eventually persuading us to buy a Buddhist calendar pendant at half the price first asked. It took me a few days to be able to haggle confidently, but the children were delighted with our bargain, and the boy was no doubt equally pleased with the final price.

We seemed to have arrived in Nepal on washday. At every street corner, beside temples and shrines, even on the temple steps, groups of women were squatting, rubbing and scrubbing over large traditional earthenware and copper pots, buckets, even saucepans, tipping the dirty water into the gutters where, in theory, it would run away, and fetching clean water from communal pumps. Goats were herded between the piles of washing; cows were either tethered or free to wander – one was asleep in a shrine; hens and chickens clucked and scratched, loose or in crates or under upturned baskets. In spite of the livestock and the lack of hot water, when the clothes were hung from window frames and eaves they had somehow been banged and squeezed clean. A sari draped from the top of a second-storey window almost brushed the ground. By mid afternoon even the washing hanging in streets so narrow that the warm winter sun merely cast deep shadows had dried and been taken in. When the clothes washing was finished, it was the turn of the children, who were stripped, soaped, sluiced, and dressed in an assortment of eastern and western garments. Finally, still squatting in groups, the women washed their long dark hair, flapping it dry with their hands.

The ground-floor rooms of many of the houses were open-fronted shops. In one, a man in skinny-calved baggy-bottomed white cotton jodhpurs was selling fruit, vegetables, and spices colourfully arranged on wide flat shiny leaves. Another man, similarly dressed, was cross-legged beside a pyramid of flat dishes of curd or yoghurt. At a street corner half a dozen women in saris were scrubbing a shrine of a gaudy god or Buddha, and as they passed the shrine people nipped in to touch parts of the statue and then parts of their own bodies to gain strength. The steps outside temples and shrines were being used as market stalls for shawls, blankets, and lengths of cloth, religion and everyday life mingling with no thought of sacrilege. The Nepalese have gods for everything and everything for the gods, who are fed, taken on annual excursions round the streets, represent and are assumed to experience every human emotion, virtue, and even vice. So long as the inner sanctuaries of Hindu temples are undefiled by the presence of non-Hindus, why should they object?

Driving through the narrow streets seemed hazardous. Some, too narrow for cars to negotiate, had superfluous modern signs forbidding them to try. The few drivers proceeded in a series of hoots and jerks, he who hooted loudest having right of way. The crowds parted to let them through and closed immediately behind them. Tricycle rickshaws, elaborately decorated, with a high-hooded double-seated arrangement over the back wheels, rang their bells to clear a path, serving both as taxis and as mini transport vehicles. One was pedalled past us, piled precariously with bales of cloth. Another, hung about with pots and pans and loaded with bedding, seemed to be doing a house-removal service. At a street corner we were surrounded by half a dozen of these rickshaws, the drivers all laughingly trying to persuade us to hire them. After some good-humoured banter we managed to persuade them we weren't going anywhere, and they parted to let us escape.

It was only six weeks before the coronation but the area around the Durbar Square and ancient Hanuman Dhoka temple and palace complex, where the king was to be crowned, was in a state of incredible confusion. Women in saris, which did not seem to hinder them, and men in official white cotton jodhpurs and long white shirts, made their agile way up bamboo scaffolding to the pagoda roofs of the temples, carrying great baskets of bricks. On the ground, groups of men and women were busy breaking big stones into little stones, grit and gravel, by hand. It seemed impossible that the repairs and renovations would be ready in time for the great day.

The bazaar streets led us to residential back streets closed in by the high dark walls of terraced houses. Dogs like under-nourished wolves slunk in and out of the courtyards which were the only open spaces. A signpost saying "Library" pointed through an open doorway into a paved yard overlooked on all sides by glassless shuttered windows with a great heap of rubbish rotting in a corner.

When we felt we could not absorb any more new impressions, we retreated to the hotel, to enjoy a more remote view of the city from an unexpected grassed roof garden. Beyond the tumbled jumbled roofs of the tightly packed bazaar area and the gleam of gilded pagoda temples the line of snow-covered peaks to the north divided land from sky. A vulture, like a small eagle, soared overhead. The heat of the day changed suddenly to the cold of a Kathmandu winter evening, and below us in the street faces and feet were soon all that could be seen of both men and women as they wrapped themselves tightly in shawls which they pulled cocoon-like over their heads. Sunset over the mountains was swift and dramatic and by six o'clock it was dark, the temperature having dropped from the mid seventies to near freezing.

We phoned Kanti, who was dismayed that she had not met us at the airport. "I was sure you were coming tomorrow," she said, "everything is prepared for tomorrow." The telegram we had sent a week before never did arrive. With true Nepalese hospitality, we were asked to join several other guests for supper at the Giris' house, where, as soon as we had left our shoes in a pile in the hall in deference to local custom, the children were introduced to "Cowboy", a dark-eyed lively little boy of eight, no bigger than our five-year-old Megan, and taken to have supper with him by a married elder daughter of eighteen. Kanti told us that she was not at all pleased that the daughter, a very beautiful intelligent girl who spoke excellent English, had chosen to marry so young, although her husband, a student at Tribhuvan University, was not an unsuitable match and their baby was the centre of much family attention.

As we knew that Jaya and Kanti had met less than eighteen years before and had had no children when they had returned to Nepal from England after their marriage, we were puzzled; but when the daughter told us that she had a three-day trek to reach her "other Mother's home", we were able to piece together the complicated family relationship. Jaya, we remembered, already had a wife when we first knew him, through an arranged marriage, and two children at home in Nepal. When he had then married Kanti, already a qualified doctor herself, we had wondered what would happen when she returned as second wife in seniority but first in choice. Neither Kanti nor Jaya ever mentioned the other wife to us but their relationship with the daughter of the first marriage was affectionate.

Although it used to be common practice for Nepalese men who

could afford to support them to take more than one wife, it has now been officially forbidden. The king himself has only one queen, as had his father, the first king to limit himself in this way. But there are still many families where the children of several women are all the legitimate offspring of one man, making it very difficult for an outsider to sort out the complex family relationships of the extended family, with several generations often living under one roof and uncles referred to as fathers, the oldest uncle being the senior father.

Arranged marriages are also still common, although marriage traditions vary considerably from one tribal group to another. Since it is now no longer allowed to take more than one marriage partner, these differences are less obvious than they used to be and are gradually disappearing as it becomes easier to travel and intermarry – modernization here, as everywhere, bringing with it standardization. Traditionally, in some groups, it has always been acceptable, even expected, for a woman to take more than one husband; or by marrying one to imply that she would, and should, welcome sexual advances from other males of his family; or for a man to take not only more than one wife, but also any number of mistresses, according to his financial and social status. Jaya's marriage to Kanti while he already had one wife had therefore not seemed at all strange or unusual.

Kanti herself was, and still is, something of an exception: a highly qualified professional woman in a country with very few well-qualified doctors of either sex. In most countries of the world, women who reach the top of their profession are unfortunately still in a minority. In Nepal, with the assumption that anyone of a high caste and social position has several servants, it is perhaps easier than it is in England for a woman to combine a career and marriage without guilt or tension.

The next day was a government holiday, the first day of the tenth month of the Hindu year, for which Kanti told us all the washing on our first day in Kathmandu had been a preparation. We decided to visit a temple where a ritual Hindu sacrifice was to take place, and hired a car to take us the fourteen miles to the temple of the south goddess, Dakshin Khali, leaving Kathmandu on a route which took us past the university. "It is very big," the driver told us, "five or six hundred students." It was also the only university in Nepal, opened in

1959, a few years after the present king's father, Mahendra, inherited the throne from his father, Tribhuvan, and called Tribhuvan University in his honour. Gaining a diploma or degree brought higher social status, but unfortunately it did not necessarily provide the sort of employment to suit this distinction, and within only a few years the graduate unemployment figures were disturbingly high, with over one hundred people applying for any one white-collar post.

As in many universities, political opinions did not always follow the acceptable line, and the university was all too often closed for a while because of student unrest.

An ex-student we talked to later, now a wealthy business man, told us that in his year many of his fellow students had been arrested because of their political opinions, and said that a high proportion of students were very critical of the regime. In a country where political parties were illegal, this did not go down well, and there were still an unknown number of political prisoners in Nepal.

Not far from the university, we passed a large new German-built cement factory, standing idle because of a shortage of the raw materials for making cement. Lack of limestone was one of the reasons for the factory's inactivity: although it was next to a lime kiln, apparently no one had thought of asking if the kiln operators would provide lime; they wouldn't.

We were soon winding up steeply between the terraced fields we had seen from the plane, and which were to become a familiar part of the scenery and remain one of the overwhelming visual impressions. The temple of Dakshin Khali lay at the bottom of a long flight of wide dilapidated stone steps in a dank dark hollow overshadowed by trees. The steps were lined with stalls selling bangles and various highly coloured spicy delicacies on leaf plates, and strong sweet tea served in glasses. Although the sun was hot and bright, it did not penetrate the trees round the tiled temple courtyard, enclosed by railings and built out over a river. On a second flat area beside the temple courtyard, sacrifices were being skinned, gutted, cooked over wood fires and eaten. It was all very communal and informal. Family groups brought their goats and hens for slaughter, tethering them to the temple railings, coming and going with heaps of spices and titbits on shiny leaves to offer the goddess. The animal to be sacrificed was sprinkled with holy water, shaking its head to indicate that it accepted its fate. It

could not be sacrificed unless it had nodded its agreement, but as most animals will shake their heads if water is sprinkled into their ears, this was easily arranged.

We watched one sacrifice, not the clean sharp blow immediately severing the head which we had expected. A goat was held firmly between the legs of one man while another slowly sawed off its head. The goat struggled frantically, giving every appearance of having changed its foolish mind. Megan was very upset, hiding her face against my legs and saying, "It's too sad; the goat hadn't done anything wrong." The fresh blood was smeared on the goddess, spattering freely over the tiles. Mangy dogs wandered in to lick it up and were beaten off. Barefooted women in saris and men in cotton jodhpurs slopped round in the blood carrying out their rituals, then the slaughtered animal was washed in the river ready for skinning and cooking. Ill fortune for the tenth month had been averted and stomachs were soon filled. We disappointed our driver by saying we did not wish to stay any longer; I felt that we were intruding on a form of worship which we could not fully understand.

Hindu Nepalese make sacrifices on feast days and at religious festivals throughout the year, in much the same spirit that we eat vast artificially fattened turkeys at Christmas, but whereas in western countries we buy our meat already killed, they combine the symbolism of offering it to the gods with the practical purpose of killing to eat. Their's is perhaps a more honest approach. The children accepted the logic but, having a British sentimentality about all animals, were upset at the practice.

Religious rituals of blessing, often involving sacrifice, are known as *pujas* and performed even on inanimate objects. An English pilot, Harry Haynes, in Nepal to train local pilots, described to us a puja performed on a new plane the king had acquired. A buffalo was killed and its headless body carried three times clockwise around the plane while the blood spurted out and was smeared on the fuselage. The ceremony would be repeated every few months, the gods satisfied with the blood and the ritual, and the meat cooked and eaten. The practice of human sacrifice has now been abolished, although it is rumoured that it is still carried out every ten or twelve years at one village, Harisidhi, only a few miles outside Kathmandu. Animal sacrifice is practised only by Hindus, as the taking of life is contrary to Buddhist belief – although Nepalese Buddhists eat meat which has been killed by other people, as we do.

On the way back to Kathmandu, we stopped in a village of elegant but dilapidated two-storey brick and timber houses arranged round a stagnant pool. Giant stacks of sweetcorn raised on stilts, like huge swarms of bees, reached to the carved overhanging eaves. Little orange and lemon bushes and large spiny-edged flat-leaved cacti formed a boundary along the road. A girl, barefoot and dusty legged, stood watching us, one arm behind her back to support a baby. She looked about six, but was probably nearer twelve. When we tried to talk to her and take her photo, her commercially minded elder brother appeared, demanding payment of one rupee and a cigarette – smoking being very common, even among quite young children. Apart from these two, the village was deserted, the inhabitants having probably walked to Dakshin Khali to sacrifice and make puja.

That evening we transferred all our luggage to the Giris' house on Ram Shah Path, a straight, wide, relatively modern road lined with a mixture of old buildings and visually unattractive twentieth-century houses of the modest desirable residence variety. A brass plate showing Kanti's medical status was fixed to a high wall through which a gate led into a grassed garden. In the hall a line of patients was waiting to see her when she returned from her day's work at the hospital, where she was senior obstetrician, as well as acting as the queen's consultant gynaecologist.

Medical facilities were still available only to a minority, with one doctor to every 33,000 people and few hospitals outside the valley, although there was an increasing network of health posts. The only medical training available in Nepal was for diplomas in health, hygiene, and some other ancillary medical services. There being no medical faculty at the university, both Jaya and Kanti went abroad for their training, to England and India.

Very few women could expect to have any medical attention for childbirth, the survival of mother and child being largely a matter of chance. In many areas, it was still the custom to isolate the mother completely for ten days after giving birth, as she was considered unclean. A family who could afford to do so would hire a woman of a lower caste to look after her and prepare her food, but a poor or low-caste woman would have to look after herself during the time of "birth pollution". The infant mortality figures we were given ranged from 20 per cent to 50 per cent. Even for those who survived the first few years of infancy, life expectancy was still little more than thirty-five years. For the wealthy it was, however, possible to obtain good medical treatment. The next day Kanti brought a timber merchant home to lunch. In the morning she had delivered his wife of a baby at the hospital – he was one of the minority who could afford to pay for this privilege, and his baby therefore stood a higher chance than most of surviving.

Kanti's timber merchant friend came from the Terai, the flat fertile area along the south of Nepal which was until recently malarial jungle. Apart from an area retained as a game park, most of this jungle had been cleared and its particularly virulent form of malarial mosquito virtually eradicated. The Terai was able to produce enough food on the new farmland to export, but as it was physically almost impossible to arrange transport to the hill villages in the north where this surplus was badly needed, most of it was sold to India. Although the timber merchant spoke with sorrow of the destruction of traditional ways of life in the Terai, he seemed to be living very comfortably, deriving considerable income from the exploitation (his word) of the remaining forests. He told us of the Dhimal people, one of the few groups able to survive in the malaria-ridden jungle but now dying out and forsaking their ancient traditions. "The women used to wear a single cloth under their breasts, but now they have dropped their topless fashion for saris to conform with other people. They were happy-go-lucky people, living on fishing and farming; when one village had food they would beat their drums as an invitation to other villages and everyone within sound of the drums would come and join in a three-day feast," he told us. His English, like that of most educated Nepalis, was fluent.

When Kanti left to go back to the hospital, and the timber merchant to attend to urgent business affairs, we made our own way down into the town to change money at the central bank, a confused and dimly lit hive of activity, with armed guards at the entrance and dozens of employees scurrying up and down stairs with ledgers, or sitting behind wooden counters. We had to queue at three separate counters, first downstairs, then upstairs, then downstairs again, while our passports were checked, we were issued with crescent-shaped tokens, and finally received twenty-five rupees to the pound for our travellers' cheques in exchange for the tokens.

We had been invited to dinner, with Kanti, by her neighbour, Mrs Sushila Thapa, a large and formidable lady in her forties who was then assistant minister of health, rising briefly to minister a few months later. The minister of power was among the guests, but even he could do nothing about the frequent power cuts which punctuated the evening. The first power station serving the valley was installed as early as 1906, but the supply was erratic and feeble. In spite of improvements to the system the wiring in many houses was still old and inadequate. Mrs Thapa was trying to run two fan heaters as well as lights but each time the second heater was switched on the lights fused.

Sushila Thapa had risen to her high position through her own determination, which was rare in a country where name and connections still counted more in gaining promotion than ability or suitability for the job. Although the Rana stranglehold had ended, there was a constant battle for power among top families, sometimes one, sometimes another, being in favour. Sushila Thapa was born of peasant stock, married at thirteen, and could be called a self-made woman – but within a year or two of the coronation had ceased to be minister. She was first elected to the Rashtriya Panchayat, the central government, in 1964, and by the time we met her had already been on, and even chairman of, committees dealing with foreign affairs, health, broadcasting, education, and national development, her various duties having taken her to a dozen countries and made her one of the most widely travelled members of the government.

Her English was excitable and the more enthusiastic she became, the more her thoughts rushed into words while we talked with her, the more difficult she became to understand; but she was determined to talk to us directly and not through someone else – not a lady who easily took no for an answer, or was pushed around.

Only two months before we met her, Mrs Thapa had been visiting one of the village health posts, on horseback, and was knocked off her horse by a branch, the fall breaking her back. Health posts supplying only the most rudimentary treatment, with no doctors or surgical equipment available except at a few scattered hospitals, she had been carried for eleven hours before anything could be done for her injury. In spite of this, she was already fully active and as energetic as ever, having made a remarkably swift recovery.

We found this story particularly alarming, as we were leaving to trek the next day ourselves, and would be equally far and on occasions considerably further from any medical aid. Our doctor in England had supplied us with a basic medical kit, including antibiotics, but these would not be much use if one of the children were to fall. We had already been told another story to point out the danger we were exposing ourselves to: an English woman had fallen off a narrow path near the Annapurna sanctuary, which we were aiming to reach. She had been unconscious and one of her companions had had to walk for two days to fetch help from a mission hospital at Pokhara.

2

On Foot to a Tibetan Camp

Our flight to Pokhara, in a small plane seating twenty people, left Kathmandu only half an hour late the next morning. The airport was crowded when we arrived as another flight had been held up for an hour and a half. Delays on internal flights are frequent and inevitable, and caused not by inefficiency but by climate and geography. It is often foggy in the early morning, even in the dry season, and pilots have to wait for the sun to burn off the mist before they can take off. Flying time at some of the smaller mountain airstrips is limited to only a very few hours a day because of strong winds funnelling through the valleys from the mountains.

On a clear day the hundred-mile flight from Kathmandu to Pokhara is one of the most poetic in the world: soft smoky-grey cotton wool clouds drift in hollows and valleys, masking the contours of rock and man-made terraces and softening the crystal-sharp snow peaks of Annapurna, Dhaulagiri and Machhapuchhre.

Although we had obtained trekking permits from the Kathmandu Tourist Office, where an official sat at a desk surrounded by passports and paperwork, we had made no arrangement for porters or a guide. Within a few minutes of landing on Pokhara's rough grassy airfield we were approached by a Tibetan who led us along a dusty road, past shanty shacks selling a colourful array of unhygienic but tempting local food, to his little square trekking office. He looked at our luggage to assess how many porters we would need – each one would be prepared to carry a maximum load of seventy pounds – and had soon arranged for us to hire a young Tibetan guide, who spoke fluent English, as well as Tibetan and Nepali, and was to prove an invaluable interpreter and friend for the next fortnight, and three porters whose English was limited but who lived up to the Nepalese reputation for unfailing cheerfulness. We were to pay Sonam, the guide, thirty rupees a day (£1.20) and each of the porters half that amount for carrying our luggage in baskets on their backs, taking the strain on thongs across their foreheads. Although we felt guilty at asking other people to carry our belongings, we could not have managed to carry everything for the children and ourselves, and had we done so we would have deprived the porters of at least a temporary income. Tourism is now one of the most important sources of income in Nepal, and there is little other paid work available in the hills.

While our porters shared out our luggage, we paid a brief visit to Colonel Jimmy Roberts, who started the first trekking organization in Nepal Mountain Travel, in 1965, after his retirement from the army. He had first climbed in the Himalayas while the Ranas were still in power in Nepal, was later military attaché to the British Embassy in Kathmandu for a few years, and in 1963 undertook the organization of 900 porters engaged to carry the gear for an American Everest expedition. This experience, and his fluent knowledge of Nepali (not to mention Hindustani), were put to good use when he started his service to trekkers and mountaineers, at the same time giving employment to a number of "Sherpas" as guides and porters.

Looking every bit the retired English army officer, with a friendly red face and baggy British shorts, he made us welcome at the pheasant farm he had set up when he retired from active involvement with the successful Mountain Travel service. The bird-rearing enterprise wasn't going too well just then, he explained, as most of his buildings had been burnt down. Fortunately his thatched bungalow had escaped the fire, and in several of his long wired runs a variety of exotic-looking Nepalese birds were still strutting around. Poinsettias, thirty feet high, were splashes of red above his thatched roof, and mango and kapok trees gave shade to the runs.

Because of the huge variations in height which give Nepal such a wide variety of climate and therefore of vegetation, the country has somewhere or other almost all the birds, apart from sea birds, found anywhere in the world, including all sorts of pheasants and other birds reared elsewhere as game. Jimmy Roberts was the first person to rear these birds under controlled conditions in Nepal and was anxious to make sure that his efforts helped to preserve them. An interesting sideline was the sale of quails' eggs, a great culinary delicacy, to a

Kathmandu restaurant. The eggs which were not served up to wealthy and discerning guests were returned and hatched out.

After a leisurely hour chatting with Jimmy Roberts, we returned to the trekking office, where Sonam and the porters were waiting. Although we could have taken a bus or taxi through the town, we decided to start as we would have no choice but to continue – on foot. It was very hot as we walked through the main street, past open-fronted shops, booths, stalls, and houses varying from the elegantly carved to mere shacks. Tailors were sitting at ancient treadle machines in open doorways; bullock carts loaded with bricks manoeuvred laboriously between dilapidated hooting taxis. The road led gently uphill, until it passed the last houses and became a wide flat grassy track between drystone walls leading north above a stony river bed.

Brightly painted lorries loaded with rock passed us on their way to and from the furthest point where motor traffic was possible: a stone quarry cut into the hill. We had to wait for a lull in the quarrying before we could walk safely along the path below. Boys high on the cliff face were throwing stones until they caused a minor but alarming and noisy avalanche of falling rocks which bounced across the grass. When enough had fallen, they were collected and loaded by hand to be taken back to Pokhara, to be pounded, also by hand, into gravel and grit.

Our destination for the first night was Tarshi Pahlkiel, a Tibetan refugee camp and Sonam's home. We had asked him how far it was and been told "three hours". We soon realized that this was the only way to measure distance, as a mile may, very occasionally, be flat, but is more likely to involve walking steeply up or down several thousand feet, the steepness and roughness of the path determining the time.

As we approached the camp, spread out on a wide flat grassy area above the river, Megan said, "Mummy, I don't feel we've been walking a long way." I hoped this would last, as she was too heavy to carry. Many of our friends had reacted with horror when we had told them we expected a five-year-old to walk for several hours a day in the Himalayas. At first, the porters offered to carry her, but soon accepted that it was a matter of pride to be able to tell her grandmother she had walked all the way. We encouraged her by telling her she was the youngest trekker ever to have walked so far, which was probably true.

The camp was a collection of mainly single-storey houses, many white-washed, arranged round an open grassy space, and neater and cleaner than many Nepalese villages, with running cold water from a communal tap, a cold water shower, and hole-in-the-ground toilet cubicles – luxuries we did not appreciate fully on this first day of our trek.

Sonam showed us round the two centres of the community: the carpet factory, and the Buddhist temple. In the factory, semi-automated looms were clacking away, mainly operated by women working an eleven-hour day, who took their babies and young children with them. They were weaving traditional Tibetan designs, the thick hard-wearing pile skilfully trimmed by hand. A generator made it possible to continue production long after dark.

Outside the low white-washed monastery, beneath long white prayer flags (Megan called them "prayer rags") fluttering from tall stripped poles, a group of elderly women were prostrating themselves on the steps as they wailed out their prayers. It was gloomy and smelled of incense inside the building, where very small monks, some no more than five years old, were sitting cross-legged, chanting under the leadership of an aged senior monk. We were proudly shown their large modern prayer wheel, made in 1974 from an old oil drum. The idea that by spinning a wheel prayers could be sent up to heaven appealed to our children; if the efficacy of the prayers is in proportion to the size of the wheel, the faithful at Tarshi Pahlkiel should be assured of a good position in the next life. Tibetans are Buddhist, as are many Nepalese, although the official religion of Nepal is Hinduism. Both believe in reincarnation.

This camp was one of several set up to solve the problem of an influx of thousands of Tibetan refugees after the Chinese invasion of Tibet – which the Chinese prefer to call a liberation, maintaining that Tibet was always part of China, a belief not shared by the Tibetans. In 1950, the Chinese invaded (or liberated) Tibet, drawing up a seventeen-point agreement; refugees crossed the border into Nepal. But Chinese rule was uneasy, and in 1956 it was admitted that there had been fighting between Tibetans and Chinese. In 1959, the Dalai Lama, the spiritual and political leader of the Tibetan people, left the country for India, claiming that the Chinese had violated the 1951 agreement and had been brutal in their suppression of both religious and political freedom. Chinese troops again moved in, and more Tibetans left rather than live under Chinese rule. Since then, very few outsiders have been allowed into Tibet, although those who have been able to visit the country report that living conditions have been considerably improved.

The northern people of Nepal are in many ways more Tibetan than Nepalese, being mainly Buddhist and living at the same altitude and under the same physical conditions; but food in the villages was already in such short supply that it was impossible for the thousands of refugees to be easily assimilated. The aid of another traditionally neutral mountain country, Switzerland, was enlisted, and camps set up. In a short time, the Tibetan carpet industry, founded under Swiss supervision and with Swiss financial help, became the first organization in Nepal to export.

Sonam's family was typical of those who fled from Tibet, which they left in 1959 when he was five years old. His parents did not like to speak of their escape and the next few years spent in the northern Nepalese territory of Mustang before settling at Tarshi Pahlkiel, although like most Tibetans in exile they hoped one day to be able to return.

Although the camp at Tarshi Pahlkiel had every appearance of permanence, its inhabitants remained refugees, with little contact with the local Nepalese population, except through business interests. Sonam told us that they were not allowed passports, the only restriction he felt strongly, as he would have liked to travel to America and England. They could not, he said, hold official positions, and were looked down on by many of the Nepalese. Although official government policy claimed to be working towards total integration, many Nepalese used the word *Bhote*, meaning Tibetan, as a term of abuse.

Sonam's father worked in the camp shop, and his wife in the carpet factory, where he also worked occasionally when he could not find employment as a guide. A highly intelligent younger brother would have liked to go to secondary school in Pokhara, but the family could not afford to support him; he had already started doing a "little business", like many others at the camp – buying and selling, trading somewhat suspect Tibetan temple antiques and curios, with a sophisticated and convincing turn of sales talk often backed up by heart-rending but not necessarily accurate hard-luck stories. Alistair was easily persuaded by a boy of his own age to buy a "valuable old ring", actually a small coiled spring.

Although many of the younger people spoke fluent Nepali, and some English which they learnt at the camp primary school and from tourists, the older generation seemed not to bother or wish to learn the language of their host country. The camp hostel was run by a tall good-looking man in, I guessed, his thirties, who spoke no Nepali but some English, falling into a middle-age group in the camp. He was interested to hear that David had once interviewed the Dalai Lama and wanted to hear every detail of their meeting again and again.

The two-storey hostel, with an outside staircase leading to a row of dormitories furnished only with plain hard wooden beds and candles, served both as tourist accommodation and as a stopping place for the many Tibetans still trading along an old route as far as the border. There was glass in the dormitory windows, a luxury when everything not produced locally had to be carried. With money very scarce, not surprisingly, glass window panes come low on the list of priorities in most villages.

Tibetan noodles and thick pancake bread, and *chang*, their cloudy bitter-tasting beer with a strange granular texture which David enjoyed and I found undrinkable, were served in a separate single-storey dining-room with a corrugated iron roof and heavy wooden shutters in place of glass. By six it was dark, and a heavy but short rainstorm was loud against the closed shutters and on the roof as David and I sat by candlelight writing our diaries, while the children and Sonam swopped card tricks.

By eight-thirty, there were heavy hints that it was bedtime. Our sleep was disturbed by the eerie ghost-like howling of jackals, whose eyes could, we were told, be seen gleaming outside the stone wall encircling the camp when they came in search of food on winter nights. By six the next morning, the first early rays of the sun were creeping across the mountains. We sat up shivering in our sleeping bags to watch as the light stole from peak to peak until the summits of Annapurna and Dhaulagiri stood clear and bright while the dawn glow edged across the sky. As daylight replaced night, there was a steady trickle of barefooted men and women carrying loaded baskets on their backs along the grassy path past the camp. By eight o'clock, after breakfast of tea and pancakes, we too were on our way, with, Sonam told us, an eight-hour walk ahead.

3

Some Gurung Villages

Officially, all people in Nepal are now considered equal; in practice, it takes more than a statement of government policy and a few years of development to wipe out centuries of caste distinction. The caste system, which came to Nepal with the Hindu religion from India, sets people on a social ladder and makes it very difficult for them ever to change their position. The social and religious idea of caste and status is further complicated by the existence of tribal groups, many of them once distinct mini-nations, which can perhaps best be compared with Scottish clans; but even this comparison is misleading, as there are often subdivisions within the group which are themselves like the clans, and which have a clearly defined position in the caste system of their tribe.

Many of these groups, or tribes, have maintained their individuality, largely because of the difficulty of travelling from one area to another or even from one village to another; the customs and beliefs of one tribe often still differ greatly from those of a neighbouring tribe, and it is therefore impossible to make any general observation about the way of life in Nepal as a whole from a knowledge of one area. We pestered Sonam with questions about race, caste, customs, and beliefs, and whenever we met people who spoke English or could persuade Sonam to interpret for us we tried to find out more about local customs and the differences between tribal groups.

The first village we came to after leaving the Tibetan camp was a scruffy straggling little place called Hyanja, according to Sonam inhabited by very low-caste people of the Guine tribe, a people about whom I have found no further information. But "They keep pigs; only low-caste people keep pigs," Sonam told us. The pigs were dark-skinned bristly hogs which looked as if they could be dangerous if annoyed, although they were lying quietly in the shade of some trees.

As we approached Hyanja, a minstrel with a slight squint came out of one of the houses and walked with us for almost two hours along the flat almost dry river bed, playing mournful songs on a two-stringed fiddle. Groups of chattering children passed us on their way to school in Pokhara, in no apparent hurry as they sauntered across little paddy fields which would be flooded in the summer by monsoon rains. The minstrel left us at Suinkhet, a cluster of shacks surrounded by a few trees in the middle of the valley and inhabited by a group of semi-nomadic Thakali people, who lived there during the dry months, providing refreshment for travellers, and then in the wet season moved up into the hills, returning to the valley at the end of the monsoon to rebuild their houses and re-establish their business.

In the village café, little more than a shack but cool and clean, we were given rice, dark speckled dahl, and tiny gritty river fish the size of cooked minnows, which we ate sitting on rough wooden benches. A huge basket of chillies stood on the earth floor, and jars of coloured pickles and spices lined simple shelves against the wall. Through the open door we could see the steep slope up which we were about to climb out of the valley. Oval and round thatched houses were perched precariously at intervals all the way up, surrounded by incredible tiny flat terraces carved out of the hillside and green with winter wheat. We all found the walk up several hundred steps cut into the hill tiring. At times the drop beside us was almost sheer and the path itself little more than a stone ladder slanting slightly from the vertical. We could see why the local people carried their goods in baskets on their backs so that their hands were free to help them climb.

At mercifully frequent intervals, about every half hour, we sank down at a resting place, or *bussoni*, a two-tiered square platform built of blocks of stone, the lower level at pack height so that a loaded basket or heavy rucksack could be hooked off on to it and picked up again without any stooping or straining. In the centre of each bussoni was a large tree, the only trees never to be cut for firewood, planted in honour of a dead relative, usually by a son on the death of his father.

At last the path evened out a little at a bussoni on the edge of a scattered Gurung village, with hedges of bougainvillaea in full flower separating the houses. We watched a man absorbed in his task of making a new basket, sitting cross-legged on the grass; a boy looking after a dozen sheep and a woman with a basket on her back, suspended by a strap from her forehead, watched us from a cautious distance. Several other children gathered, and one told us that he was in the fourth grade at school, very proud that he could speak to us in English; the others became braver when we shared some chocolate with them. Alistair started to climb the shade tree, but as none of the local boys joined him we told him to come down, afraid he might be showing disrespect.

We were already about 3,000 feet higher than Pokhara, but still had to go down a little and up a lot before we reached our stopping point, the Gurung village of Damphus, where many of the houses were again circular and thatched, arranged in terraces a little apart from each other beside steep tracks of hand-hewn stone steps converging in the centre of the village. Megan was very tired but summoned enough energy to run the last hundred yards to the village guest house on a steep grassy slope, below a grove of trees which we were told was sacred. The house, entirely made of mats and rough thatch, with bundles of bracken stuffed into it here and there and a rough framework of timber, seemed to serve as a local meeting place, and a changing variety of people crowded into the one room, 10 feet wide and 30 feet long.

Eventually only we and the inhabitants were left. They turned out to be two women, neither of whom was married, a boy, the son of one of them, a bundly black puppy called Kali (Blacky), and a couple of dozen hens, which were shut into a crate for the night next to our sleeping space. Supper, which with all the activity had taken a long time to prepare, was eaten in relays – we were first, with Sonam, then the porters, then the inhabitants – partly because of a shortage of plates, and partly because many Nepalis still feel that they are defiled if they eat with strangers, one of the many taboos attached to the Hindu faith. The cooking was done on a baked clay platform built around a floor fire, rather like a giant sandcastle, halved by a metal bar.

The women juggled skilfully with saucepans, burning embers, and fresh wood; all Nepalis seem to have a genius for lighting and keeping alight fires, picking up burning sticks and twigs which would have taken the skin off our fingers, blowing almost dead cinders into life through metal tubes, and apparently not bothered by the smoke, which has no way of escaping as the houses are always built without chimneys – in the monsoon a chimney would be a weak point, as the rain pouring down it could easily wash away the less substantial houses which are often built of unfired clay or, as this one was, of mats and thatch. Strips of buffalo meat were hanging from smoke-blackened beams to dry, and we were given some of this, tough but tasty, with our rice and some sort of chopped fried greens.

At 6,000 feet, it was a cold evening, with a gentle hill drizzle finding its way through the mat walls and thatch. Tucking the children up in sleeping bags on the floor, David and I sat round the fire, edging nearer and nearer to the embers for warmth. The porters, whom we called Curly Bill, Peter, and Solti, the Nepali equivalent of Mate (their true names being difficult for us), huddled close together under a shared blanket – with none of the inhibitions about physical contact with a member of their own sex which are felt in western society. Our hostesses did not seem to feel the cold, although they had bare midriffs between their cotton sari skirts and short-sleeved tight-fitting tops. Their few possessions were stuffed between the beams and thatch of the roof, and most of their money must have been spent on jewellery. In the usual manner of Gurung women, they wore heavy gold earrings not only on the lobes of their ears but all the way up them, and nose ornaments, having had both ears and nose pierced in childhood. As most people in the hills seemed to have perpetual colds, wiping their noses across the backs of their hands at frequent intervals, I felt that those nose rings and ear studs must have been most uncomfortable.

Gurung women have a reputation for friendly bantering flirtatiousness; although we could not understand the backchat between these two and the porters, they were obviously no exception. Between banter, they sang mournful Gurung songs and we chatted with the porters, whose ambition was to join the Gurkhas, preferably in the British army, as this was the highest paid employment a hillsman could hope to achieve. They told us they belonged to the Magar people, many of whom had served in both the British and the Indian armies, and called themselves Pun Magar, or members of the Pun clan of Magars. Solti was stocky, broad-faced, shy and simple, infinitely gentle in spite of his strength; Curly Bill, taller and wirier, had unusually thick curly hair, most Nepalis having smooth sleek hair, and was always ready for a practical joke or a game; Peter was older and more serious and the only one of the three who was married, returning to his family when he could not find work as a porter. Communication with them was difficult, because of the lack of a fluent common language; but they were patient with our halting attempts at basic Nepali, and spoke a little English.

Many of the villages in the middle hill area below Annapurna are inhabited by Gurungs, fairly high on the national social ladder although not quite on the top rung. Damphus was the first of several Gurung villages we stayed in. Although some Gurungs have moved down to the fertile Terai since it was cleared for farmland, the majority still live on the southern slopes of the Annapurna Himalaya. Many Gurung men have served in the British army's Gurkha brigade or in the Nepalese or Indian armies, and so have been able to bring money into their villages, spending it to improve the standard of living. In spite of having travelled during their military service, it is unusual for the men to marry outside their own people.

In some ways, Gurung society is freer than that of many other Nepalese people. Young people are, for instance, free to choose their own marriage partners, and widows are allowed to remarry, which some tribes forbid. Boys and girls have plenty of opportunities to meet and get to know each other, through a system of youth clubs, known as *Rodi.* A rodi is a group of a dozen or so young people, who spend much of their time together from the age of ten or eleven until they are sixteen or seventeen. The boys and girls of a rodi have the use of two village houses, where they sleep during the dry months; although the sexes are segregated (officially, anyway) at night, during the day they work and fetch wood together and even go on joint outings. When a young couple decide to marry, they tell their parents, and go back and forth from one set of parents to another until they have a baby; then they marry and usually settle in the paternal home, the bride's parents providing a dowry in kind.

The round and oval thatched houses we had passed on our climb up from the valley were typical of the Gurung style of building; they also build rectangular houses, of irregular blocks of stone, cemented together with mud, which is used mixed with water as a cheerful clean-looking colour wash, white, yellow, ochre, or a rich red-brown, on both inside and outside walls. The stone houses have long verandahs along the front wall, opening on to paved courtyards, and may be slated or thatched. Terraced houses are unusual, as they like to space themselves out, although together the houses of a Gurung village, usually on or near the top of a slope, form a compact cluster of anything from a few dozen to as many as 700 houses. Sonam told us that many Tibetans had been assimilated into Gurung communities, as their customs and attitudes are similar, Buddhism being the traditional belief of both although many Gurungs now officially belong to the Hindu faith, or adopt a mixture of both.

We asked for breakfast before we left Damphus in the morning, and were given omelettes and tea. It wasn't until we had eaten that we realized that there was now no food left in the little house for either our hostesses or the porters, and we hoped that the guest house stocks could be replenished from the money we paid for our bill: fifty rupees (£2) for a substantial evening meal for six – the porters providing their own food – eleven eggs, twenty-two cups of tea, and several kettles of *rakshi*, the local ale, brewed from millet and often drunk hot.

Our first hour's walk after leaving Damphus took us through wild cherry woods, up steep rock steps on loose shale and across deceptively clear mountain streams. Megan, who found the shaly uphill path and steps tiring, was thirsty. "It's mean that we can't drink the water when we want a drink so badly. It looks clean enough," she complained, but this was the one health precaution we were determined to adhere to. Although the water in the mountain streams looked so clean and pure, there was never any guarantee that it had not been contaminated higher up, and above many villages there might be a sheltered fall or pool used as the local wash-place and toilet, there being no facilities of this sort in village houses. But we did fill a thermos flask with water to which we added some sterilizing tablets, and which we drank at the first village we reached, when we stopped for the porters' mid-morning brunch break. A group of Gurung men were working on a new and solid house in the style of a group of stone two-storey buildings, cutting the rocks to shape by hand. The hand-hewn wooden door and window frames, and plain wooden eave struts and roof supports, were already in place. Some small boys were playing marbles, with stones, but our children were too shy, and too tired, to ask to join in the game.

Refreshed by the water and the rest, we walked on for several hours through more woods, carpeted with small bright blue violets, bushes with brilliant blue berries, and shrubs like a cross between philadelphus and rhododendron, from which fibrous fawn paper is made. The air was heavy with the strong sweet smell of their tiny white flowers. We had crossed several mountain streams before, coming down a steep slope, we reached our first bridge, a plank between two long tree trunks slung high above a boulder-strewn fast-flowing river. An ingenious hollowed-out log aqueduct carried water from a stream high across the track of a second stream.

We stopped for the night at the Gurung village of Landrung, a well-organized and relatively wealthy farming community high on a slope above a deep river valley. The rectangular stone houses, some thatched and some slate roofed, with carved and even painted frames and struts holding up verandahs and roofs, were the most substantial and elegant we had seen. We were made welcome at a house cut into the hillside so that the long verandah at the front, where baskets and rolled mats were stored, was one level higher than an open barn filled with heaps of straw at the back. Thatched animal shelters in the paddy fields near the house looked stronger than the guest house at Damphus. In the paved courtyard in front of the house, elaborate ricks of sweetcorn on stilts were covered with mats, with straw bird-scarers like corn dollies on the ridge. Several mother hens were imprisoned under upturned baskets, so that their chicks could come and go through the mesh but would not stray too far. Immediately we arrived, a group of local children, thinly clothed in spite of a cool wind, gathered round us. Many of them had scabby weeping cold sores, and most had running noses. Quite young girls were acting as nursemaids to very small children, who clung, bare-bottomed, to their backs, like baby monkeys. A young woman, deaf and dumb since birth, made most explicit gestures as she tried to work out our family relationships and the ages and sex of the children.

Inside, the house was dark and spacious. The main ground-floor area, where we were given mats to sleep on, was divided into two rooms by a mat screen; a solid open-runged wooden staircase wedged between the front and back outside walls led up to the family's sleeping area. Off our sleeping place was a store room, where huge earthenware pots of provisions were stacked, and a separate kitchen and eating area, a long narrow room along the back of the house, suspended over the hillside and supported by the wooden uprights of the barn. A fine display of gleaming pots and bowls and a large red radio, on which David tried, but failed, to get the BBC Overseas Service, were visible signs of the household's wealth and social status.

We had already admired a fine buffalo, warmly bedded down on straw in a stall alongside the house, and were offered buffalo milk and curd with our supper. Megan appreciated this, as the vegetables with our *dahlbhat* – rice and dahl – were hotly curried. This was almost the only time on the trek that we found fresh milk, and even here it was not used for butter or cheese, although buffalo cheese, hard and light-coloured and richly flavoured, made at a Swiss dairy, could be bought in Kathmandu. In the hill villages, buffalo, cows, and goats or, above 10,000 feet, long-haired yaks, have to survive on such a meagre diet that they rarely produce much milk. Cows are allowed to multiply and wander in the villages, being sacred creatures which it is forbidden to kill, their sole practical use being the production of manure, usually the only available fertilizer. Buffalo and goats were, as we had already discovered, killed for meat and sacrifices.

Four generations lived together in the house. A young man had had his head shaved bald except for a little wisp, in mourning for his father. Gurungs either cremate or bury their dead, and observe a thirteen-day period of "death pollution", during which the relatives of the deceased may eat no salt; mourning lasts for six months or a year, and no meat or liquor may be taken until this is finished. The final death rites are performed a year or even longer after death, several families often combining for this ceremony, in which food is taken for the dead and a lamb of the sex of the deceased sacrificed.

Apart from the outward sign of the shaven head, the family did not appear to be grieving deeply. They offered to sing and dance for us, but asked twenty rupees, nearly a pound and a lot of money by local standards, for the entertainment. Sonam made it clear that he did not approve of the family's commercialism, a side effect of the increase in tourist traffic. We suggested that we should do a cultural swop; we had recorders with us, and would sing and play our own traditional songs in exchange for their songs and dances. They said they would not understand our songs; we said that we would not understand theirs, but would like to hear them. Sonam offered to translate. Eventually we played and sang, for nothing; their children tried our recorders, with much laughter and squeaking as they blew; but they were adamant about being paid; we became equally stubborn, and so we did not have the pleasure of their entertainment.

The village we were to walk to next was hardly any distance away, but separated from Landrung by a deep steep valley. We had a choice of two routes, one long and gentle, the other straight down a thousand feet of shallow rock steps to the river, the Modi Khola, and accepted Sonam's decision to take the shorter route. The steep walk down made our legs tremble, and our calves felt like jelly as we took short careful steps, to avoid the painful complaint known as "Sahib's knee" which can be caused by attempting to stride downhill, and tried to copy the porters' rapid almost mincing walk which comes naturally to the hill people and does not jar the knee.

By the time we reached the Modi Khola, we were all exhausted; but worse was to come. First, there was the river itself to be crossed, on a precarious log bridge thirty feet above incredibly clear bright blue water, swirling round huge boulders and only still in deep darker blue pools between rocks. Garlands of faded marigolds and little straw figures were strung across the bridge in welcome to spring. Although it was high above the winter water level, the bridge would be swept away by the monsoon rain later in the year, and have to be rebuilt after the rains. Once over the bridge, it was a steep thousand feet up to a welcome tea-shop, level across the narrow valley with Landrung. The tea place was a mat hut, next to which a wood-framed square stone house to replace it was half-built. In the unroofed new building, with thick solid walls two feet high, a group of women and children were drying their hair in the wind, hanging their hands down and flapping and slapping at the wet hair as we had seen the women of Kathmandu do on our first day in Nepal. It was only 10 o'clock in the morning, but we had already walked down and then up the equivalent of a whole English mountain and were ready for several glasses of tea and a mid-morning breakfast omelette. Nepalese omelettes have a flavour and freshness I have never managed to achieve, even with our own free-range eggs. They are cooked in a very small pan, each egg broken, beaten and cooked separately, so that the result is a cross between scrambled egg and omelette, with nothing added, and particularly delicious after several hours of walking on an empty stomach.

The rest of the way to Gandrung, a larger Gurung village than

Landrung, was up – up – up. I imposed a total ban on talking while walking uphill, as Megan's constant harking back to school and her friends in England demanded answers my lungs were incapable of giving if I was to keep going. "Mummy, do you know what Mrs Rees said? ... and somebody pinched my rubber. It wasn't fair, was it? – Mummy, I said it wasn't fair, was it?" Perhaps not; who could care as one heavy foot was raised ahead of the other, up foot after foot until we were 2,000 feet above the river and 1,000 feet higher than our starting point. Beside a bussoni, as the granite steps at last changed to sloping grass, were three square stone Buddhist-style temple towers, or *chorten*, in honour of the dead.

We were only fifteen or so miles from Annapurna, and stopped at a guest house called after the mountain which dominated the view. The Annapurna Lodge, a two-storey building used to catering for tourists, actually had beds, hard wooden-framed and based with no mattresses, in a first-floor communal guest dormitory. The stairs leading up to the bedroom were wedged unevenly between the back and front walls of the main downstairs room, which was both the guests' dining-room, with a wooden table and chairs, and bedroom for the owners, who slept on a long wooden bench against the wall facing the door. On a rickety card table upstairs, we found an empty tin of Panda Chinese condensed milk and a pack of cards; a large poster of Edinburgh was pinned to the wall.

Although the walk had been taxing and seemed long, it was only just after midday so we had time to explore the village, walking along narrow lanes between terraces of neat stone houses, each with its own paved courtyard and long ground-floor balcony, arranged in tiers cut into the hill. It was bitterly cold, the wind funnelling down from Annapurna and along the valley and eddying up to a promontory of sheep-nibbled grass nigh above the river. The village school stood on this draughty promontory, with a steep drop down on three sides of the playground. As we approached, we were immediately surrounded by children, who all looked very small and cold beside our three, although several were older than Jane. Gandrung was a fairly wealthy village, with many ex-Gurkhas whose pension money had been used to pipe water through long polythene tubes draped from house to house, but the children were dressed in a ragged assortment of tattered garments, clutching shawls or even towels and teatowels left behind by trekkers round their thin shoulders. All were barelegged, and most barefooted, in spite of the bitter wind, and their calf muscles, developed by constant mountain walking, bulged from skinny brown legs. Several had cold sores, the scabs weeping, and a distressingly large number suffered from thickly catarrhal running noses.

They tried their English, which they learnt at the school from the age of eight, but in spite of great goodwill on both sides it was difficult to carry out a coherent conversation. Although it was their lunch hour, we were dragged boisterously into the school's walled courtyard, with open-fronted classrooms on two sides and a two-storey building with doors and windows facing the arched entrance. Each of the open classrooms was furnished with benches and tables, and raised slightly off the ground. In theory, all one hundred and eighty children in the village of primary school age should have attended full time at the school; many did not, as their labour was needed at home and in the fields; very few went on to the nearest secondary school, in Pokhara, a day's walk away by the most direct route, as few families could afford school fees and accommodation costs, or the loss of child labour which further education would entail.

Walking back from the school, feeling like a family of Pied Pipers as many of the children followed us, laughing at our strange names and clothes – they found Megan particularly amusing; she found their attention rather overwhelming – we met three of the teachers, whose English was good enough for us to enjoy a long conversation until we were all shivering in the wind. They told us that not all the school's eight teachers were fully qualified. The government was trying to increase the scope and education in the country, but had to rely on unqualified teachers to staff many schools. Anyone who had had any secondary education could teach, although official policy laid down that in future only trained teachers would be employed. These teachers were worried about their own jobs, but it would take many years before there were anything like enough teachers to go round. One of them told us he came from Pokhara, where he had been at school and at training college; his salary was £300 a year, from which he had to pay for board and lodging; but he had not been paid at all for several months.

Two eagles swooped down near us, one carrying some small unidentifiable prey in its thick curved beak. We had already seen a number of vultures, not the scraggy sinister creatures the name evokes, but elegant beautiful birds, at first sight easily mistaken for eagles themselves. This was our first close view of the king of the air in flight, and we watched for a while as the pair – king and queen – soared effortlessly, chasing a pair of less graceful vultures from their territory. Alistair attempted in vain on several occasions after this to take pictures of eagles in flight, but they were always too swift, although they often came within a few feet of us.

Later in the day, following the sound of drums drifting up a lane between the walls of houses enclosing us on either side, we were welcomed into the courtyard of a large house, where a group of children and men were dancing under a mat awning. The boys were wearing flounced brightly coloured skirts and gemmed crowns, necklaces, and ear-rings, and the girls skirts under divided drapes, with gold scarves over their heads and chunky coral and turquoise beads heavy round their necks. The men were playing tabla-type drums. The dance form was stylized and simple, but at the same time complex and graceful, obviously following an ancient tradition, with elaborate oriental hand movements and repetitive rhythmical foot movements, the right foot always kept flat, the left pivoting regularly on the ball.

Mats were spread on the ground, and we were beckoned to sit down. A silver plate was placed before us; on it were grains of uncooked rice and a lighted candle. One of the teachers, who was among a group of adults watching the dance from the verandah, explained that a month-old baby boy was being christened. We were expected to put money on the dish in front of us, a gift to the baby made by each of the guests. Putting in ten rupees, we found ourselves the centre of a heated and incomprehensible discussion. The teacher, embarrassed, told us that we were felt to be mean, as being English we must be rich. We added another ten rupees; this met with approval. The baby's parents would expect to raise between 200 and 300 rupees for their child in this way (£8 to £12 – quite a significant amount in a country where the average income was counted in tens rather than hundreds of pounds), the same ceremony being carried out for both boys and girls.

Enormous acrid garlands of marigolds were put round our necks, and we sat on the ground watching the dancing for another hour before there was a brief halt for refreshment. Scaldingly hot and highly spiced "tea", more like curried broth, and crescent-shaped pastries of rice dough filled with hotly flavoured chopped buffalo meat, were passed round. After the broth, rakshi was poured out liberally from a kettle; then the dancing started again, this time less formalized. It was obvious that the gathering would not break up for many hours, so, cold from sitting for so long, we took our leave, wishing the father of the baby good luck. He was a respected and senior member of the community, the local *panchayat* secretary – the equivalent of an English Parish Council chairman, elected annually for a maximum of three years in office.

By the exit from the courtyard, the baby's grandmother was busily weaving, in spite of the festivities, and demonstrated for our benefit. The ends of the threads were attached to a carved stone set permanently in the ground. Weft and woof controls were of shaped wood, and with another roughly carved piece of wood each row of weaving was pushed tight against the previous one – a slow and painstaking process. We had already seen many people wearing shawls in the simple traditional pattern she was making, with narrow red thread woven in stripes on a plain background. A buffalo stood watching with apparent interest, and a gaudy cockerel strutted in and was shooed out.

Supper at the Annapurna Lodge was served by candlelight at the table in the dining-room, which, as it had no fire, was cold. The smoke but none of the heat from the kitchen fire floated in through the open door, so when we had eaten we asked if we might join our hosts on the kitchen floor. The hotel was owned by a widow and her son, one of the school teachers, who did as much of the work as he could manage as his mother was not strong. Unlike most of the people in Gandrung, these two were Brahmans, and conscious of their superior social status as members of the highest caste.

A ten-year-old Chetri girl, higher caste than the local Gurung people but lower than her employers, acted as their servant, working early in the morning before school and returning to finish the hotel chores in the evening. Proudly, she showed us her school English book, from which she had learnt as little of our language as we knew of hers. We conducted a two-way conversation lesson, pointing to parts of our body or of the kitchen and telling her the English words, which she repeated carefully, telling us the Nepali equivalents. Even with this limited selection of words, the common Indo-European root of both languages was apparent – *nac* for neck, *panz* for five, *dui* – two, *saat* – seven, *das* – ten.

The kitchen was clean and well kept, but smoky even at fire level. The walls and floor were painted with orange slip, renewed at least once a week. Pots and pans were stored on shelves after they had been cleaned with earth and water, and the rakshi kettle was put on the embers. We allowed the children to sample some hot rakshi – *tato raxi* – which had an almost instantaneous effect on Megan, who became very giggly and woke me in the night to go out to pee. Outside, it was crisp with frost under our bare feet, with the mist swirling eerily in brilliant moonlight, the stars bright in the gaps.

Next morning, the light was sharp on the mountains; we all woke at 6, except Megan, who slept on as we opened the shutters, letting in draughts of ice-cold dawn air. Again, as we had done at Pokhara, we sat up shivering in our sleeping bags to watch with delight as dawn crept across the clear pink-tinged slopes of Annapurna and Machhapuchhre, which means Fish-Tail; we could pick out its distinctive shape from the other peaks. "How many hours is it today?" we asked Sonam as we left. "Oh, only three or four," he answered vaguely.

The sun was soon hot and the morning frost cleared early, as we were on the sunny side of the hill, dawdling for a mile between terraced houses where pumpkins, corn, hay, mat rolls, were neatly stored on the wide overhanging verandah roofs. For some time we kept stopping to look back at the tiers of village streets and paddy fields sharply silhouetted against the haze of the hills behind. Just outside the village, we passed a man squatting in a little field, surrounded by heaps of dung which he was slowly spreading by hand. Dung is often also used as fuel, and dried in pats against outside walls. Soon we were scrambling across a bleak boulder-strewn hillside, cut by tumbling streams. Little mat-roofed wood and stone shelters had been built above falls over water-driven grain mills; when these were in use the main stream was diverted through the mills along hand-cut channels.

The hillside looked like a lunar landscape, eroded on a vast and tragic scale by generations of intensive cutting of wood for fuel and foliage for animal fodder. Only a few stunted bushes had been left on the great scree slips, and in several places recent rock falls had obscured the path and covered the laboriously cut steps we were following uphill. When we asked village people if they were aware of the problems of erosion, and whether they had a system of replanting to replace what they had cut, they spread their hands helplessly. Yes, they were aware of it; and in many villages they had to walk further and further to fetch wood for their fires and food for their livestock; but what could they do? They had no money to buy seed or fertilizer. They had to have wood to cook on, and their animals must be fed, and so they carried on cutting and chopping, carrying great weights in their baskets for longer and longer distances, looking like bowed walking forests.

It was rough going over the heaps of boulders, high round the end of the hill to cross a stream which widened to an unbridged river lower down the slope, and up round the next slope, nearer and nearer to Annapurna, which gradually disappeared behind another hill. A tea house on a high ridge sold cigarettes, biscuits, and rice by the handful from huge sacks – all of which had had to be carried from Pokhara. A family-planning poster was displayed, the shop doubling as the local health post. Farmyard picture-book cockerels with gleaming gaudy feathers scratched hopefully round our feet. At last we were walking downhill, through a moist cool forest of stunted shrubs and tall twisting rhododendrons in bud. The ground was scattered with minute delicate mauve primulas as the path wound down a slope too steep for even Nepalese farmers to attempt to terrace it into fields. Near the bottom, on a sandy almost vertical track leading to a river bed, we had to stand aside as a buffalo was coaxed and bullied up to a solitary smallholding. Beside the river, a narrow fast flowing channel through stones and boulders which would be swamped by the summer rains, a group of men and women were sitting outside a mat tea house, splitting cane to finish a new mat for the verandah, and chewing sugar cane.

On the other side of the river, we had inevitably to walk uphill again, at first on a twisting path on a one in five gradient; then although Sonam had promised us a flat stretch, the path merely flattened out enough to continue straight uphill without the twists and turns. Megan was put as family leader for the first 2,000 feet in an effort to keep her moving, as she had been so slow earlier in the day that she and I, chatting about this and that to fill the time, had been left behind and had only known which path to follow by the distant sound of Sonam's cheerful whistling.

Clouds were drifting down the hillside; above us a snowstorm powdered the mountain slopes and floated on to leave a sprinkling of white on the hilltops. The clouds round Annapurna were dark and heavy, and the peak only occasionally visible. Eagles soared overhead. Just above the village of Cchomrung, the last permanent habitation before Annapurna, in a deep valley under the mountain which cast an almost permanent shadow, a school lesson was being conducted in the open air, the children clustered cross-legged or squatting on the grass repeating droning lessons. A new school building was half-way to completion, a village work party singing and laughing as they built the walls.

The minstrel who accompanied us along the valley near Suinkhet

Below: Near Pokhara; Machhapuchhre behind the house

In the family kitchen at Landrung, with three generations. The fireplace and cooking ring are typical of hill houses

Below: High up on the path from the river between Landrung and Gandrung. Megan, me and Solti

Alistair crossing a log bridge

Below: A village woman and child. Baskets are used for load carrying in the hills

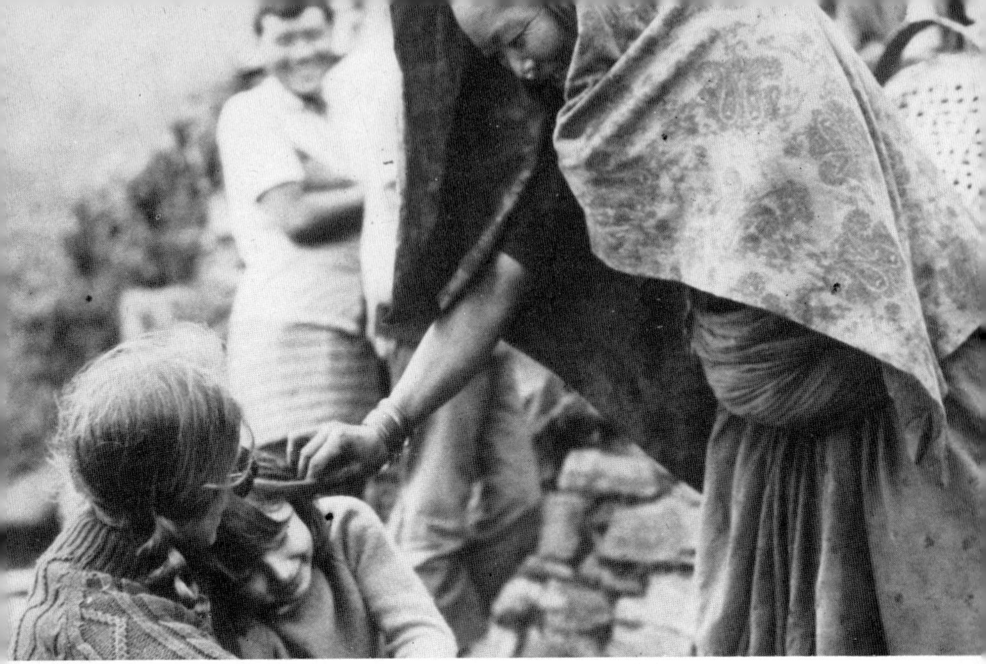

Gurung woman near Gandrung, intrigued by Megan's fair hair and skin. She carries her belongings in her cummerbund

Megan with the schoolchildren at Gandrung. In the background are the houses terraced up the hill

Alistair with the leading mule of one of the mule trains at Gorepani; the leaders have red head-dresses and large bells; many mules also wear valuable decorated saddle-cloths, like the one with its back to the camera

On the way up Poonhill from Gorepani to watch dawn over the mountains

The view of Gorepani (9,300 feet) from Poonhill (10,000 feet)

The view from Poonhill at dawn of Machhapuchhre, the Fish Tail Mountain

Mule train at a staging post set up by Thakali people. The mule train has just arrived and the mules are being unloaded for the night

4

Under Annapurna

The only place to stay was a dilapidated windowless mat house pretentiously called the Hotel Cchomrung, where the porters would have to sleep virtually outside under the mat awning of a narrow verandah in front of the sole door. Fortunately the storm threatened by the rain and snow clouds over Annapurna would hit the other end of the house.

A couple with two very young and sickly children were attempting to run the hotel, with no help, and seemed to have been overwhelmed by the tough conditions which most village people cope with cheerfully and efficiently. Although the husband had spent ten years in the British army, he did not seem to have achieved much in the way of improvement with his army pension, apart from a token gesture to western ideas of sanitation: a mat screen round an uncovered stinking toilet trench and rubbish pit a few yards from the house. This was the only place at which I ever felt at all depressed, even, I suppose, a little homesick. Everywhere else we went, the people were friendly and cheerful, so used to their way of life that its hardships were not so much accepted as not noticed; but this couple had known another life; they had returned to Cchomrung with dreams of improving their lot, and were just not able to climb out of the squalid trap of poverty, inefficiency and ill health.

The sight of glowworms, little phosphorescent pinpricks of light against a low dark stone wall, cheered me. As night fell, the clouds came so low that if we stood up our heads were in swirling damp mist. Suddenly the hillside across the path was lit with flames. Men and boys sprang from hummock to hummock, shouting through the combined concealment of mist and smoke, as a fire shot up the slope. They were preparing the pasture for spring grazing in the method of their ancestors, by burning off dead grass and bracken to allow the new growth to push up with more nourishment for the animals. It was a dramatic scene, creating an isolated patch of life and colour; the crackling scrunching sound of fire almost drowned the constant background noise of water from the river running through the village and the tumbling streams and falls rushing down to it from the hills all around.

Inside, beside an excessively smoky fire, we would have liked to help the wife with supper preparations, but for once could find no way to communicate with her, our efforts at Nepali and sign language being ignored. The children, an undersized toddler and a baby of eight months, bare-bottomed and whining – the first crying children we had met – crawled dangerously close to the flat open hearth. Many Nepalese children are permanently scarred by burns from unguarded floor-level fires. My sleeping place on the floor was so close to the embers that I did not dare turn over in the night and was woken soon after five when the woman relit the fire to cook rice and hot milk for her husband before he set out on his monthly trip to Pokhara to draw his army pension. There was no breakfast for us, and a cup of tea was grudgingly given.

Although we had planned to continue up to the Annapurna Sanctuary, the snow line was unusually low and we were ill equipped to camp for the night at Hinko, the only shelter, a cave some hours' walk away on the summer mountain pasture, where Sonam told us that he had once been snowed in. It seemed foolhardy to risk this happening to us, with children, little food, and no mountaineering experience. We decided instead to spend a gentle relaxed morning exploring off the beaten track, and try to reach one of the many waterfalls on the slopes surrounding the village. Solti volunteered to come with us, leaving Curly Bill and Peter in Cchomrung. Sonam never even thought of staying behind: we were his responsibility, and he took his duty of taking care of us very seriously.

"This will be an adventure," we told Jane, Alistair and Megan. The adventure started gently enough, with a scramble between spindly trees and through tangled undergrowth. The ground was littered with boulders from rock falls as we climbed, not too steeply, until we were several hundred feet above the village. There was no path, which we should have realized was ominous: the Nepalese do not leave slopes uncultivated, ungrazed, untrodden, without good reason. By the time we had scraped and scrambled our way up to a rock-based clearing some five or six hundred feet above the village, we still had not had the sense to realize this. We were halfway up steep falls, which cascaded over widely spaced boulders from a thousand feet above our heads to the river bed as far below. Sliding down the rocks for sixty feet, to a colossal almost flat boulder wedged across the falls, we looked down nearly a thousand feet of vertical river. There were occasional splashes and minor hesitations as it met the obstruction of a rock or a root, but the central part of the fall was quite uninterrupted, sheer, fast, inexorable.

On the left of the falls, across the water, we could see no further than the first impenetrable bank of trees; looking forward, over the valley, we could see first down to the glistening snaking river then, as we slowly raised our eyes to the steep hills the other side of the valley, the tree line ceased and Annapurna proper began. To our right, or in other words, the direction in which we wanted to go, it was impossible to see far ahead, as the whole hillside was jungly wood. But above us and to the rear, it looked equally thick and tangled and already it was impossible to see where we had forced our way through.

"If we work our way down through the trees, we can get back to the village along the side of the hill and we won't have to retrace our steps," I suggested. It seemed sensible enough. At first, it was easy to go steeply downhill by aiming from tree to tree; the idea was to hold on to a tree, pick out the next one to be reached, leave go of the first and make a few slithering rushing steps until the lower tree was clasped in a bear hug. The trees were close enough together for it to be difficult to miss altogether, as with arms outspread one or other hand was bound to meet a tall narrow trunk.

We scrambled downhill like this for a while, crabbing slowly sideways at the same time, feet always at an angle so that they could be used as brakes; then it became so steep, and the ground so treacherously covered with loose dead leaves, that the only safe way to continue was by sliding on our bottoms, grabbing hold sometimes of a trunk and sometimes a protruding root. Fortunately, there were neither nettles nor brambles to catch us unawares but even so we were soon badly scratched. After our steep slithering into what seemed an endless wall of trees, so thick ahead of us that no sky could be seen through them although we knew that there was sky ahead, we tried to work further round the hill for a while. The undergrowth was even thicker than on our way to the falls, and Sonam and Solti went ahead, slashing a path for us with their sticks.

At last, walking on such a slope that one foot was making its own parallel path at ankle height to the other, we began to see blue sky ahead of us between the trees, and hurried on along their newly threshed path to catch Sonam and Solti. Sonam met us, retracing his steps, looking worried. "Be careful," he warned; another few steps and we saw why: we were on the edge of a sheer drop; the trees had given way to bamboo and ivy running in a narrow band along the top of a cliff stretching as far as we could see in the direction in which we had to go; above us, the roots seemed to be the only thing holding the hillside in place, as that too was now almost sheer, and so tangled that to walk in it would be impossible.

What were we to do? If we stepped out over the cliff edge we would drop at first into space, then break our fall many feet below on the tops of more trees; if we jumped out a little way instead of merely stepping over the cliff, we would probably fall to the valley bottom, so steep was the hillside. The thought of retracing our steps was unbearable: and in any case, we doubted if it would be physically possible. It seemed equally impossible to go back, to go forward, to go up, or to go down. If only, we thought, with the advantage of hindsight but without the comfort of having survived our self-inflicted ordeal, if only we had had the sense to realize that the trees were too thick and crowded ever to have been cut for firewood – and that had they been accessible they would undoubtedly have been cut.

The only way to go on was by alternately sliding and swinging out over space, with only bamboo roots to hold on to as we lurched from handhold to handhold, retreating a foot or two into the undergrowth to catch our breath again after each swing out. Megan was often unable to reach the next handhold, and at first I helped her, holding on with one hand myself while I swung her with the other arm across a gap, catching my breath each time until she had pulled herself into a safe position by a root, where she clung on until I joined her. But for a five-year-old she was excessively heavy, and after a while I was too exhausted to take her weight; we sat miserably in some roots, not daring to move. The others had left us behind and we couldn't even hear them, although as we had heard no screams or crashes we assumed they were safe.

At this point, I must admit I was afraid. What, I couldn't help asking myself, would happen if I tried to carry Megan across another gap and found I could not hold her? My relief was great when Solti reappeared beaming beside us. He had left his basket ahead and lifted Megan on to his back, showing her how to cling on tightly without choking him. Immensely strong and agile as a monkey, he swung effortless from tree to tree while I struggled along behind him, and in a few minutes we had joined the others on top of a large flat rock.

Unfortunately, the hill above the rock was a sheer wall; the rock itself, a huge boulder perched and blocking our way, overhanging the drop to the valley bed, was straight-sided and perhaps twenty or twenty-five feet high and at least as wide. A twisted rope of ivy roots stretched round it, and this was our only handhold while we inched our way, one at a time, to the other side, using grooves or uneven patches in the rock face as footholds. Meanly, we made David go last – being the heaviest, he was the most likely to break the twisted ivy handrail and cut us all off. It probably took only minutes, or even seconds, for each of us to negotiate this obstacle, but it seemed like hours before we were all sitting on grass on the village side of the rock, at last on a gentle slope again, in a clearing not far from the start of our ordeal. Near us, some boys were cutting wood; they pointed out the way back to the village, and when we offered to share some chocolate with them were enthusiastic in their acceptance. "Would you like some chocolate?" we asked. "We VERY like," they answered.

It was surprising to find that our whole adventure had taken only a few hours. Megan was upset that she had been carried, but we told her it did not count as it had been an emergency. As far as we know, we are the only foreigners to have reached the Sara Falls – or whichever falls they were: no one seemed quite sure – but made a vow to stick to well-defined routes and tracks from then on. Peter and Curly Bill said they were glad they had not come with us, but after a morning in Cchomrung were eager to leave.

We broke the walk back to Gandrung at the mat tea house beside the river below Kimrung, where the children, David, and I, insisted that this time we would sleep outside allowing the porters the limited floor space inside. There were glowworms on a wall near the river, and when I woke in the night soft drizzling mist hid the hills and swirled visibly along the valley and under the mat awning, and was damp on our faces.

When we came into Gandrung next day, having managed the steep track up through the woods surprisingly quickly, we felt as if we were returning to friends, and were delighted to resume our conversation with five of the teachers who were drinking tea at the Annapurna Lodge in their lunch hour. They told us that their Panchayat, or parish, stretched from Cchomrung and included nine villages. Its members were elected from the villages, and a Panchayat secretary was elected to be their representative at the district Panchayat in Pokhara. The district Panchayat in turn sent a representative to the Rashtriya Panchayat, the government, in Kathmandu. At all levels, party politics were forbidden, and the king had ultimate control of the Rashtriya Panchayat, of which he chose a number of the members himself.

Individual panchayats could apply for local facilities such as clinics. The nearest clinic, or health post, to Gandrung was, the teachers told us, "not far away", by which they meant only a few hours' walk, and a health visitor came to the village every week or so, but only the most basic treatment or advice was available locally, and even that was not always free. The nearest qualified doctor was at Pokhara, where there was a free government hospital; but the standards there were not high, and it was advisable if possible to raise the money to go to the mission hospital on the edge of the town.

There was apparently very little political awareness in the village, which without the advantages of radio, television, or even the press for information was not perhaps surprising. I never saw a newspaper in a village, and only one or two radios, and the centre of government in Kathmandu seemed totally remote to village people who were never likely to go there, and many of whom referred to the valley as "Nepal" as if it was a separate country. Moreover, as indulgence in party politics was forbidden, although there were people in the villages who were critical of the regime and were at the time particularly resentful about the coronation expense, they dared not voice these opinions openly. The majority of people in the villages knew and cared little about the coronation, their minds and time being fully occupied with their own struggle for existence. Few government officials visited hill villages unless they were particularly conscientious or the villages part of a prize development project. We had already discovered that people in Kathmandu disliked the idea of trekking, and found the foreigners' enjoyment of this chore as a holiday relaxation frankly astonishing.

We asked the teachers what they would ask the king if he were to visit Gandrung. The answer was immediate and unanimous. "We would ask him how we could improve life in our village." They said that the king had once been there, by helicopter – for about four minutes; but as a young man, we were told, he had made a strenuous effort to get to know the people and problems of the country he would later rule, trekking incognito. Perhaps the formulation of a series of government five-year plans reflected a greater understanding of and concern for local problems than under any previous ruler, but nothing could be done quickly in a country so lacking in trained experts and money, and with such impossible geographical conditions.

Everywhere we had been conscious of the vast waste of water power, harnessed only for the ingenious and beautifully made corn mills. We asked the teachers about hydro-electricity, but they were vague and unaware of the possibilities, or of the fact that for over twenty years a United Nations project to harness Nepalese water power to supply not only Nepal but the whole Indian subcontinent had been shelved because of difficulties in relations between Nepal, India and China.

The Brahman teacher-hotel proprietor, whose English was the best, at first sat quietly in the shadows, but gradually relaxed and became the most outspoken. He felt strongly that the increase in tourism was beneficial, not so much because it brought in much needed money, but rather because of the chance it gave the local people to meet and understand people from other countries. "They will learn from seeing other people, their clothes, their customs. It will broaden their outlook," he told us optimistically. Hippies, though, were a different matter, and had done much to damage international relations. "They are bad; they take food and drink and do not pay." It was, he said with feeling, not uncommon for them to run up a bill of 30 rupees, a lot by local standards, then say "Sorry, we can't pay," or "We've only got twenty rupees." This he felt was an abuse of the traditional Nepalese hospitality and courtesy; we fully agreed, and were glad that we met very few people who would come into this category.

In the evening the little Chetri servant girl again brought out her English books as we sat on the floor round the fire. The Brahman teacher joined us, standing by the door as if poised for flight. His looks were quite different from those of the local Gurung people, darker, with much thicker hair, rich black and almost wavy, and an intense brooding expression contrasting with the broad, cheerful, open expressions of his neighbours. He told us he was studying English, alone, by post, for a BA degree, but with no hope of ever going to England, or even indeed Kathmandu. He would never be able to afford to travel or study abroad, he said, and would not be able to obtain permission to leave the country without the necessary money; and anyway his mother needed his help at the hotel. We invited him to visit us at home, but "It will always be impossible" he told us, without bitterness.

He asked us to help him with a translation passage, which included several words and concepts which he said he did not understand. This was hardly surprising; the passage was from a highly sophisticated Third Programme talk by Harold Nicholson. The theories of Jung and Freud, psychological and psychoanalytical terminology, and unfamiliar western inventions such as sellotape, TIM, electric blankets, and escalators, were equally hard to explain.

5

Mule Trains and Mountains

Our breakfast of rice porridge and tea was interrupted by the arrival of an American Peace Corps volunteer, a young Texan from an enormous cattle ranch who told us he was trying to introduce Jersey cross-breed cattle able to produce milk as well as manure on the limited local diet. He was also, he said, in charge of setting up a sheep dip north of Kathmandu, and was on his way to look at an existing dip on the Annapurna summer pastures. After three months in Nepal, working chiefly on an artificial insemination project, he felt himself an expert on Nepalese farming problems, and described the government's five-year agricultural projects, the first of which had concentrated on crops and the second of which was about to start and was aimed at improving stock.

He spoke adequate Nepali, which he was at pains to show off by issuing peremptory orders to our host and hostess, whom he otherwise ignored, and talked disparagingly in English about the local people as if they could not understand. He either did not notice or did not care that Sonam and the Brahman teacher had taken an instant and obvious dislike to him. They had already told us that they did not like Americans, whose brusqueness and brashness they found insulting and which often jar on the gentle formal friendliness of the Nepalese, although the American Peace Corps has made valuable contributions to many aspects of Nepalese development.

It was cloudy when we left Gandrung at eight, on one of the pleasantest mornings of the trek, neither too hot nor too cold, for once on a flat wide grassy track which was refreshingly comfortable underfoot. For several hours we saw no one, and passed only occasional isolated houses, although paddy fields rose above us and dropped into the mist below. We were walking in the clouds, which drifted and swirled, obscuring all but the path in front, then parted to tempt us with visions of distant floating disembodied peaks which we could easily believe, as do many Nepalese, to be the homes of the gods. Soft misty veils were swept back in layers to give a glimpse of one valley, then of another, the hills seeming almost to move with the constantly changing land and cloud scape.

Gradually the sun won its battle to break through the mist and disperse the cloud. By midday it was hot, with a clear blue sky. A layer at a time, we shed parkas, sweaters, shirts, until we were wearing only jeans and short-sleeved cotton T-shirts, and very glad to reach a higgledly-piggledy village, Sarki Yong, on a steep slope, where we could rest and have a glass of tea. The village women were doing their washing at a central communal pool near the temple, and wet clothes were spread to dry along stone walls dividing the village street from the courtyards of the houses. A little girl cuddling a tiny biscuit-coloured puppy in her arms came up to us; but when we stroked the puppy, she burst into tears and clutched it tightly, convinced we were trying to take it from her.

This was one of the rare occasions when we saw any display of affection for a dog, or indeed any animal, although there were dogs everywhere, usually mangy-looking curs, howling at night and apparently neglected by day. We had found our own attitude to dogs changing rapidly, from British sentimental affection to rage and frustration at being woken by their howling, and even to fear when they approached us, and we were soon throwing sticks or stones at any which approached us in case they might be rabid. A bite from an infected dog would almost certainly have proved fatal.

Beyond Sarki Yong, the grass and paddy fields gave way to a rocky sun-drenched lunar landscape, with trees and scrub somehow finding roothold. Falls and tumbling streams cut through the rocks, and soon there was no shade at all as we climbed. High upon a wide flat grassy space, with clear mountain views, a group of thirty or more people were sitting on the ground under the wide branches of a single tree, engaged in an animated discussion about the problems of supplying water to their village, a group of houses we had just passed. They had to carry their heavy water pots some distance uphill, and wanted piped water; a government grant had been given which should cover half the cost, and this informal outdoor parish council assembly was trying to work out some way to raise the rest of the money, 3,000 rupees (£750). An ex-Gurkha explained the problem to us, but we could think of no helpful suggestions.

At another village, further along on the side of the hill, we saw beehives, made from lengths of tree trunk about 2 feet 6 inches long and a foot across, hollowed out and hung under the eaves of some of the houses. The bees were left to build up the comb inside, and destroyed each year when the honey was taken and the inside of the hive cut out and strained to remove larvae and young bees – a wasteful process, as we tried to explain by describing our own modern hives. Exotic birds, the colour of rich red velvet, flashed in and out of tall trees.

As we approached our destination for the night, Tirkhe Dunge, the terraced village houses looked deceptively grand, built into the side of the hill above a river, the Bhurungdi Khola, so that they were three storeys high at the back but only two at the front, with first-floor balconies along one dusty narrow street. This was the main thoroughfare for mule trains to and from the north. We had made a detour off the direct trading route, so had not seen these colourful trains before, but from then on were to hear the bells of the leaders in the distance and have to share the path with the mules in tens and even hundreds.

Until the closure of the Tibetan border, the mules were used for trade between Nepal and Tibet. Although trade had dropped considerably since the Chinese closed the border, Tibetan and Thakali tradespeople still travelled regularly from Pokhara to Jomsom, in northern Nepal, a journey of about ten days. We had hoped to be able to trek as far as Jomsom, in the province of Mustang which adjoins the Tibetan border, but had been refused permission to go so far north. "There was a problem; now there is no problem; but you cannot go there," we had been told firmly at the Kathmandu trekking office.

In the summer monsoon months, when the rains would wash away many bridges and make it impossible to travel any distance, the mules would be rested, returning with their owners to their homes in the north and moving south again at the end of the rainy season. Each mule was worth about £400, a considerable investment, and carried about fifty pounds of salt, rice, potatoes, or cloth in packs on its back.

The leaders wore huge bells round their necks and tall red waving plumes on their hands, and many had elaborately decorated and valuable saddle cloths.

Until it was nearly dark, and again in the morning from first light, the mule trains walked in single file through Tirkhe Dunge. We could hear the eerie tinkling of their bells long before they came in sight. The people with them were colourfully dressed, with Tibetan boots and gypsy Tibetan features, easily distinguished from the local people. Some of the mules were muzzled, to stop them grazing on the way and holding up the rest of the train, but they plodded along the path with no attempt to stray, too weary to do more than follow patiently behind the leaders.

The house we were staying in was far from clean, and for the first time we were disturbed by rats during the night. A mangy dog came in and out, licking the supper plates both before and after the meal, but as we had to eat anyway we did our best to ignore this. No one else seemed to mind. Tirkhe Dunge was a village of dogs, which howled and barked incessantly all night.

While we sat drinking rakshi with Sonam after our supper, a little girl was squatting on the floor doing her homework by the light of one little naked wick lamp. A heap of blankets in the corner turned out to be her old grandfather, who sounded as if he was in the last stages of consumption. His alternating tearing cough and spitting up of phlegm sounded in my ear through a thin wooden partition as I tried to sleep. We woke the next morning feeling we had had little rest, dogs, rats, and the grandfather having been equally disturbing. As we were expecting to return to Tirkhe Dunge in a couple of days, we lightened the porters' loads by repacking and leaving some of our belongings stacked in the corner of the room we had slept in. This we could do quite safely, as the Nepalese are traditionally as honest as they are hospitable. After a cup of tea, we set out for the longest climb of the trek – up over 5,000 feet, from the river at 4,000 feet to Gorepani at more than 9,000 feet.

The bridge over the river was a swaying but safe suspended contraption, strong enough for the children to enjoy running backwards and forwards over it a few times before starting the serious business of climbing several thousand steep steps. This, to our surprise, we managed to do in only an hour and a half, stopping once for breakfast of dark spicy beans at a village, Ulleri, perched scruffily half-way up. When we left Ulleri, I walked for a while on my own, first up more steps and then along a wide grassy track meandering round the edge of steep narrow paddy fields. Being alone was a luxury after the constant companionship of children, husband, guide, and porters, and the communal nights, but it was not long before we were plunging into thick sinister forest, where we again walked together, as the porters said that it was a "bad place". It was overcast and beginning to drizzle, and as we climbed the drizzle turned to snow, penetrating the trees and settling in thick slippery patches on the path and banks. It was dank, dark, damp, and cold.

The porters were soon well ahead of us, eager to be out of the forest as soon as possible. Sonam was patiently trying to hurry Alistair and Megan, who wanted to stop and play in each patch of snow. David and I greeted a traveller: "*Namaste*," we said, our hands pressed together and raised in Nepalese salutation. He answered in English, and for a while we stopped to talk with him, in spite of the chilling cold. He introduced himself as S.D. Khaki, a medical adviser in Mustang, where he had been posted for two years because his own language and customs, from Jiri in north-eastern Nepal, were similar to those of this central northern province. He told us he was on his way to Kathmandu, after waiting in vain for a week in Jomsom for a plane. Only two planes had landed in the previous month on the recently constructed airstrip; they could only land in the morning in clear weather, and stay an hour because of dangerously high winds later in the day. After his tour of duty in Mustang he was hoping to be able to return to Jiri, and had previously worked in hospitals, with both the Swiss and English.

We asked him about the mysterious problem which the trekking office official had said prevented us from visiting Mustang. He agreed with this official that there had been a problem, but that it was now solved. Raids had been made into Chinese-held territory by Khambas, members of a Tibetan tribe living in Mustang; the Chinese had requested the government to do something about the raiders. S.D. Khaki told us that there were few Khambas left in Mustang, and those that were still there were living peacefully with their families and were not involved in guerrilla activities. He said that a large number of Indian arms had been seized, and that everything was now quiet.

As we hurried to catch up with Sonam and the porters, we frequently had to step off the path to leave room for long slow mule trains, with an occasional donkey or pony among them, which passed us endlessly in both directions, slipping and scrambling on the narrow path, especially on the steps cut in the rock which were treacherous under the settling snow. Megan was convinced that the eerie almost wailing sound of the bells echoing through the trees was the voice of ghosts.

After the third long train in succession had squeezed precariously past us, we reached a steep stream just as a mule lost its footing and fell from the slippery steps into the water, remaining head down and motionless, its neck twisted awkwardly. Sonam ran ahead to shout to the nearest muleteer, and a little knot of Tibetans gathered round shouting angrily at each other. The mule's owner lifted its head from the water, but its neck was broken and he could do nothing. We headed the following mules on to the right track, while the muleteer removed the bridle and packs, which were shared between other fully laden mules, and the train continued, the accusations and recriminations of the muleteers gradually fading. Megan cried and the children were all upset by the incident. Such accidents are fortunately rare, the mules being sure-footed and their owners taking good care of their investment.

Although it was still early in the afternoon, it was almost dark when we plunged back into the uninviting forest. Snow was falling in small light flakes from a leaden sky, and we were glad to reach Gorepani in a hollow under steep hills. Gorepani means Horse Water, and some of the mules which had passed us were standing miserably in the snow, their packs piled up beside them. We were to stay in a long low building looking like a plain alpine log cabin, on the edge of the village where the trees thinned out. It was furnished with two small wooden tables each with a couple of folding chairs; a menu was pinned on the wall, and we sat drinking sweet lemon tea and discussing the relative merits of packet soup, omelette, unleavened bread and peanut butter, and chapatti and honey, eventually trying everything as a change from rice and dahl.

The hotel was run by an English-speaking ex-Gurkha and his wife, who, with no help, managed to look after their own three children as well as their guests efficiently, cooking on a separate fire in their own accommodation. They had spent fifteen years with the army, in Hong Kong, Malaya, and Singapore, where they would have liked to stay; but it was impossible, they told us, to obtain permission to live outside Nepal after leaving the army. As far as they knew, no Nepalis had stayed abroad after their army service in recent years, although it was possible that some had stayed in Burma after the war.

We asked them about the Khambas. They told us most of them were now in a settlement a few hours west of Pokhara, but felt sure there must still be some with explosives in the high hills, as it would be impossible for soldiers unfamiliar with the terrain to find and round up people who knew it so well. They said that mines and booby traps had been laid in the past, and although there had been no trouble in Gorepani, further north along the trade route the Khambas had earned their warlike reputation by attacking groups of travellers.

It snowed heavily all evening; we sat in the warm circle round the fire while an icy wind fluttered gingham curtains at the windows, which had neither glass nor shutters. Our intention was to get up before dawn to watch the sun rise from the top of Poonhill, a 1,000-foot steep hill above the village; but when we woke in the dark, a glance outside confirmed our fear that the snow had hidden the path, and we stayed huddled fully clothed for warmth in our sleeping bags on the floor until it was light enough to see.

On the hillside, the snow varied from a few inches to great drifts several feet deep. Alistair managed to be first, second, and third to fall over, but soon we were all wet, having trodden off the path up to our thighs in the soft snow several times. At the top, over 10,000 feet up and alone in the snow which no one else had marked, we were in time to watch the cold pink dawn light steal across the faces of Annapurna and Machhapuchhre until they stood out sharply, white and forbidding, blurred only by occasional cotton-wool clouds floating in a clear blue sky.

On the way down, the children found "yeti footprints", huge deep holes in the snow where they were sure none of us had walked; David said prosaically that they must be his own size 12 footprints, warmed and enlarged by the early sun, which made the descent treacherously slippery.

Back at the hut, we hung our outer layers of clothing on the beam over the fire and sat as close as we could to the heat to steam dry the rest, then spent most of the day alternately exploring the village and watching the daily outside activities, and drying off and warming up indoors. For the first time for what felt like months, we had three meals – a late breakfast of rice porridge, omelette, and luxurious coffee, lunch of another omelette with fried bread and jam, and finally supper of *dahlbat* (rice and dahl) and yet another omelette. There was an abundance of eggs, explained by a large deep litter hen-house behind the hotel. In the other villages we visited, eggs were scarce, as the hens were left to roam and scratch for their food, and lay where they pleased, and only shut in, squeezed into boxes or under upturned baskets, at night.

In the late afternoon, we went to look for the porters, who had arrived back late the night before, singing and stumbling in the snow, and been still snoringly asleep when we had left for Poonhill with Sonam. Since then we had not seen them, but found them at a house at the top of the village. Outside it was a thorn tree festooned with tattered prayer rags. Inside, Peter, Curly Bill, and Solti were playing drums and singing with two women, or "*didi*" (darling – or literally elder sister), as they called them. An older man sitting cross-legged in front of the fire, swaying from side to side and taking no notice of us, gradually unfolded himself and started a trance-like dance, with the hypnotic movement of a cobra. The dancing and drumming became more frenzied, then gradually subsided as rakshi was passed round, not, we imagined, for the first time. We left them to their pleasure; none of the porters returned to the hotel that night, and in the morning were penniless, asking us for an advance to buy their food.

On the way back to the hotel, we lingered to watch the arrival of the fifth or sixth mule train of the day. Mules mingled with buffalo on the village paths. Several women were washing up in an ice-cold and partially frozen stream. In one open-fronted house, a woman was weaving. A small pond was frozen over, and children, including ours, slid on the ice. Even in the cold, with the snow melted only in clear sunlit patches, the people were scantily clad, apart from the muleteers in their thick woollen skirts and jackets and yak-hide boots.

We were no longer the only guests, several other trekkers having arrived during the day. A trio of two wealthy young Nepali men and an American girl were passing round a pipe filled with marijuana, the first time we had been conscious of this drug, although we had occasionally caught a waft of its sickly sweet smell. The girl, who had taught English in Kathmandu for a while and was working in Afghanistan, insisted that all foreigners in the Nepalese capital were bored because, as representatives of their own countries, they were debarred from involvement with local life. Her companions were the first Nepalese trekkers we had met. One was studying western music, and the other was apparently a rich young layabout: we asked him what he did: "What I please," he replied arrogantly.

At supper time, there were fourteen of us round the fire. To make the catering easier for our hosts, who seemed quite unruffled, we all asked for the same food, except the pot-smoking trio, who issued a series of complicated and conflicting orders, clapping their hands peremptorily for more wood to be put on the fire. The rest of us found it easy enough to fetch a log or two from the pile in the corner of the room and tend to the fire ourselves.

In the evening, by the light from the flames, I read Lear's *Nonsense Rhymes* quietly to Megan. It was a tranquil scene, with the Himalayan peaks towering over us in the snow and darkness outside, the occasional howl of a dog or whinny from a mule and the sizzle of the fire the only other sounds. It was, however, not a peaceful night. Someone was always stumbling for a torch or shoes in the dark, or creaking open the heavy wooden door and letting in a blast of icy air, trying to creep out into the snow without disturbing the others.

We were woken early in the morning by the hippies, who with no consideration for anyone else were talking and rolling their sweet drugged cigarettes, but delayed our departure until nearly 9 o'clock, so that it would not be so cold in the forest. Under the trees, the snow was frozen in hard crystals, and long icicles hung from the branches. At the stream where the mule had fallen, its stiff body was still half-immersed in the water. Its tail had been cut away for the hair, leaving a raw gaping hole, and jackals or vultures had already started to gnaw or peck at its flesh. The children were even more upset than they had been when they saw it die.

Although it was downhill, it was a slow walk back through the forest, chiefly because Megan insisted on moving right off the path for every mule, and the mule trains were as long and as numerous as ever, with as many as a hundred beasts of burden in one seemingly interminable procession. A muleteer stopped and asked to swop his boots for my trekking shoes, an exchange I would gladly have made had my feet not been considerably larger than his. Some porters passed us, stooped under the weight and bulk of tables and cupboards for a guest house in Tatopani (Hot Springs), the next village on the trading route beyond Gorepani. At a clearing, we stopped to play with a baby monkey which had been adopted by one of the families living in a cluster of huts. It was light brown and at four months incredibly agile, with a pathetic human little face. Alistair enticed it on to his arm, where it nibbled his parka and his ears.

Once out of the forest, it did not seem far to Ulleri on the downhill path. Just before the village, we stopped to watch a man ploughing a paddy field, drawing a little wooden hoe through the earth by hand. Although buffalo or oxen are used for ploughing in the Terai, where the fields are flat, on the steeply tiered mountain fields this is rarely possible. By one o'clock, we were at the river below Tirkhe Dunge, where the porters plunged into a deep pool to wash. Not feeling brave enough to wash my hair in the icy water, although it badly needed it, I followed their example only to the extent of stripping off my top layers of clothing and shoes, and washing what I could reach.

By this time, we were all very hungry. There was no food available at the house where we had left our luggage, so Sonam went round the village in search of eggs, and returned with eight, which he made into an omelette to share between us, refusing to let me cook as it was his duty to look after us. He was annoyed because we were charged for the storage of our belongings for two nights, and suggested we should try to reach Birethanti by nightfall, assuring us it was all downhill.

This turned out to be a slight exaggeration, although it was indeed a fairly gentle, but long, walk, mainly just above the river, which was very clear and fast and would swell enormously in the monsoon. Boulders the size of houses had been swept downstream by the previous year's rains forming swirling eddies and deep pools, and the river bed and banks were strewn with great chunks of rock. There were lemon trees growing beside the path, which surprised us until we remembered we had started the day more than 6,000 feet higher, wearing all our clothing in the snow; by early afternoon, so much lower, we were hot and sticky in cotton shirts, carrying the layers of clothing we had removed as we walked.

An hour from Tirkhe Dunge, we walked through a small village where hand-cut channels with neat stone retaining walls or mud banks carried water from the river in a complex irrigation system to a wide area of paddy fields and through little mills. Further along the river, the Modi Khola, we stopped at Modathanti, a staging post of mat huts on a stony island bank left uncovered by the retreating monsoon. In the dry months, a group of Thakali old people, women, and children, lived in the huts while the menfolk travelled with their mules between Pokhara and Mustang, spending a night with their families on the way. Other traders were also made welcome with their mules, as this was one of the recognized stopping places set up along the trade route by the families of the muleteers for the winter months.

While we were there, a train of thirty mules came in, on their way north. Their packs were unloaded, and piled on the ground; as soon as it felt the weight lifted, each mule got down and rolled in the dust. A strange ritual was then carried out: one of the men took a little packet from a pocket inside his clothing, emptied it on to a dish, and mixed the powder it contained with embers from the fire. We were told this was incense, and was "holy, from the lama". The sweet-smelling smouldering dish was then waved under the nose of each animal in turn, to stop them straying from the camp during the night and protect them against marauding tigers from the hills, which seemed an unnecessary precaution as tigers were extremely rare in the area, and as the site was on an island between two fast-flowing branches of the river. When each mule had had a sniff of the incense, it was given a nosebag of corn, and then allowed to rest until the following morning.

6

A Thakali Village and a British Scheme

By the time we reached Birethanti we were 6,000 feet lower than at Gorepani, and felt as if we had walked from Norway to the Mediterranean. There was a cheerful, bustling, small-town atmosphere in the main street of gay open-fronted shops selling cloth, bangles, flip-flops, Coca Cola, and tinned food. At dusk, shutters were closed across the shop fronts, and herds of goats were driven from their hillside grazing by some of the village boys. Below the village, two rivers, the Modi Khola and the Bhurungdi Khola, mixed visibly, one clear brilliant blue as water rarely is, the other silky white, until the colours faded as the sun set softly over a landscape like a delicate Japanese painting, hills and valleys merging gradually in the distance. Somehow the children found enough energy to run backwards and forwards a few times across a relatively modern suspension bridge before we had our supper sitting outside on the verandah of the Good Place guest house.

The Good Place was an elaborate three-storey building round an inner courtyard overlooked by a balcony. Windows along one wall of a communal first-floor guest room with two beds were open on to a narrow side alley. The proprietor was an ex-Gurkha, a bachelor with several women employed to do the work while he enjoyed playing the part of charming host. One of the women woke us in the morning in a most unexpected and alarming way: while it was still pitch dark, well before six, she burst into the room carrying a lighted candle, shouted something totally incomprehensible even to Sonam, and went out, slamming the door. A few minutes later she returned and shouted at us again – uselessly, as we could still not understand what she wanted.

Among the shops and booths in Birethanti was one which the children found particularly interesting: a fritter, or *julpi*, stall; with fritters 25 pice (1p) each, they could afford to be greedy, and welcomed the chance of eating something sweet, as our trekking diet had been entirely savoury apart from a small carefully hoarded supply of chocolate and one tin of Chinese condensed milk. The julpi batter was forced through a cloth bag in flat circular squiggles into a pan of boiling fat or oil, and the cooked fritters lifted out to be dipped into bubbling syrup made from the sugar cane which grows on the lower Himalayan slopes. We have had similar fritters since at Indian restaurants in England, where they are called *julabi*, but none as deliciously crisp or sweet as the ones we bought steaming from the pan in Birethanti.

Most of the inhabitants at Birethanti were, our host at the Good Place told us, Thakalis, traditionally flourishing and enterprising traders, originally from Thak Khola, a valley between Annapurna and Dhaulagiri just south of Mustang where the relatively fertile hills of Nepal change to a more barren Tibetan landscape. Since the end of the last century, many Thakalis have moved away from their original territory, chiefly because of their trading interests, some to avoid high government taxes imposed in the middle of the nineteenth century in return for salt-trading rights. Others have moved away more recently to set up businesses, and there are many Thakali tradesmen in Pokhara, for instance, and even in the Terai. Many, like the Thakali muleteers we had already met, are nomadic traders. Few Thakalis now speak their original language or wear their traditional costume, having adopted Nepali language and dress. Although their religion was once predominantly Buddhist, and there are still Thakali Buddhists in the east of Nepal, they have also gradually adopted the Hindu faith.

Their success in business enterprises is largely a result of their custom of setting up a form of financial co-operative, or *Dhigur*, a group of up to thirty people, usually friends or relatives, each contributing a fixed yearly sum of money, giving anything from 100 to 1,000 rupees, to a central fund. Every year, one member of the group receives the total pool, to use as he wishes; if he makes a profit, he keeps it – but if he makes a loss, he must bear it himself. The group is disbanded when everyone has had a year as recipient. Anyone needing to raise capital may do so by forming a new group and taking the first year's money himself.

It was cooler and overcast in the morning, and as we were shielded from the morning sun by a steep hillside the main street was in deep shade. It was the day of the full moon, so the temple opposite the guest house was busy with a stream of people taking offerings of flowers in little tea pots and ringing the temple bell. A holy man with a vivid red and yellow *tika* painted on his own forehead was dabbing humbler plain yellow spots of colour on the brows of the faithful, and handing out holy twigs.

I wandered up the street with my camera. Many of the houses were substantial and elaborate, with elegant carving. In front of one a dignified elderly man was sitting cross-legged, dressed in spotless white official Nepali costume. On the verandah roof above him was a colourful array of melons and gourds. I raised my camera to take a photo of this picturesque scene, but he gestured that I should put it away. Disappointed, but not wishing to offend, I asked if I might take a picture of his house without including him. Each in our own language, we managed to communicate with a series of gestures for a while; then he took me by the arm and drew me towards the house, indicating that I should wait outside, and disappeared through the door into the dark interior.

A few minutes later, he emerged, leading a magnificent ram, which he wished me to photograph. It was obviously his pride and joy, and with good reason, the largest I had ever seen and the village stud, father of many of the goats we had seen the previous evening. As he enticed it to pose to best advantage, I must admit that I cheated and included him in the picture, and hope that this did not affect his health in any way. Many Nepalese, particularly the older generation, fear that their strength will be drawn from them into the photo, a belief which they share with other peoples – Muslims, for instance, who have always forbidden the portrayal of their leaders for the same reason.

We had to wait to leave the village while a long train of mules crossed the suspension bridge in single file. I wondered how they had managed to cross the river before the bridge was built, but a reference I found later to trade between Tibet and Nepal suggests that the mules were then used only on the northern part of the route, the packs being carried on the southern stretch by porters.

Two hours from Birethanti, we reached the village of Lumle, where the thatched houses, set well apart from each other, were brightly painted with slip colour washes. Trees in front of the houses masqueraded as haystacks, the hay bundled into the forks of the trunks and festooned over the bare branches. One of the advantages of the climtae is that things like hay which must be covered in England can safely be stored outside throughout the Nepalese winter, as except for the summer monsoon rains, the rainfall is so little and so infrequent that there is no danger of stores rotting; and of course in the rainy season the grass grows rapidly and hay is not needed.

The house where we stopped for lunch was small and humble, but spotlessly clean. Gleaming pots were displayed on shelves behind the fire area, and beyond this a mat partition screened the family's sleeping area. Strips of meat were hanging from substantial blackened beams, to dry and smoke above the fireplace, which was as usual flat on the floor but unusually elaborate, with four rings set into it over the flames; a sink had been built against the matting wall, with a polythene pipe to take the water into a ditch outside through a hole. Local people drifted in for tea and to chat to the cheerful house-proud Magar woman who prepared and served us our lunch, juggling her pots around on the rings and chopping greens, onions, and dried meat with swift deft movements. She told us that her husband, who had been in the Gurkhas, was at work at the farm school nearby, and that the vegetables came from there. A bundly puppy, little cheeping chicks, and even a gaily coloured cockerel hopped in and out through the open door.

Before walking on to the Tibetan camp and then Pokhara, we decided to make a detour and visit the farm school, a British project which we had already heard mentioned. Leaving a wide well-kept stone track, we went through a neat five-barred gate, the first we had seen, and up steep immaculately even steps. Towards the top, the path was crossed by other equally immaculate flights of stone steps and stone-flagged paths, leading to a series of severe rectangular barrack-like buildings with glass windows, an incongruous contrast to the local building styles.

Bill Eveley, the British manager, seemed pleased to see us, and invited us to have tea at his house with his wife and daughter. Bill, a confirmed wanderer who had worked on several other Asian and African development projects, was nearing the end of a two-year stint at Lumle, and keen to move on to his next assignment. His wife, Betty, was equally keen to move, as she found the isolated hill farming community offered her little companionship and stimulation, and disliked walking, so had seen little of the country. Her knowledge of Nepali was limited to the basic essentials needed to communicate on a daily level with her servants, as she said she did not like "gathering useless languages".

We were surprised to learn that the farm school had been set up with British money through the Ministry of Overseas Development, and that the people employed there were being paid by the British, receiving little by English standards but far more than could otherwise be earned locally. The project was started when the British army began to cut back on Gurkha recruitment, which had been a source of employment for a century; the king was unhappy about the resulting loss of jobs and income, and asked the British government to provide some alternative. The farm school was set up, as agricultural development seemed to be one of the most important needs of Nepal, and run initially on army lines, giving ex-Gurkhas building and labouring work. After six years as an almost military establishment, the training and rehabilitation of ex-Gurkhas in agriculture had become more practical under Bill Eveley, and the scheme was something of a showpiece.

Everyone we spoke to at Lumle was sad that Bill Eveley was not going to stay to carry through projects which he had initiated, and felt that under him the farm school had acquired far greater relevance to local needs than it had previously had. He himself was inclined to be despondent about its usefulness. In his view, the greatest need was for fertilizer, but lack of money and the difficulty of distribution to remote hill areas made it impossible to do much about this. Successful new schemes using modern farming techniques would, he feared, only serve to make the rich richer, possibly even at the expense of the poorer peasant farmers they were designed to help. He cited the example of Major Pun near Poonhill, whose glass-windowed house we had seen in the distance; Major Pun had planted fruit trees, initiated the deep-litter hen house we had admired, and made money.

In spite of his misgivings we had already seen one place where the people appeared to have benefited by work done at Lumle: the stud ram at Birethanti came from the improved Indian strain introduced by Bill, and the herds of goats in the villages had impressed us by their size and quality. The sense of breeding goats which could supply both meat and much-needed milk seemed to have been accepted there at least. Ex-Gurkhas are usually men of some local standing, and new ideas introduced by them, through their training, therefore stand a good chance of being adopted by the local community; and our impression of the Nepalese was that they were usually ready to adopt new ideas once their value had been proved.

At the same time, the traditional intensive hillside farming techniques can in many ways not be bettered; after all, the Nepalese have been surviving by farming in their own way for centuries on land which would defeat most western farmers. The chief problems we had noticed, and which Bill Eveley confirmed, were erosion through over-intensive cutting of fuel and fodder, and the loss of crops through livestock, especially holy cows, being allowed to wander freely.

We were pressed to stay the night, and offered supper in the canteen, where we were the only guests in a room capable of seating forty or more at long tables covered with oilcloth. Faded pictures of England adorned the walls. The resident vet, a young Englishman David's height (6 feet 6 inches), joined us; his immensely long hairy legs under tiny shorts reduced the children to such an impolite state of hysteria that Sonam took them to explore the farm again in the dark, and we banished them to bed early in one of the two guest cubicles. Each of these was furnished with camp beds, with the unexpected luxury of a flush toilet and cold-water shower, and, until 10 o'clock every evening, dim electric light provided by a generator.

Until long after the lights were out, David and I talked with the vet about Nepalese development. As he saw it, the chief problem was to help families on small plots to be more than barely self-sufficient and have some extra financial income. The average Nepalese family had to support itself on a plot smaller than an English football field, and in many places the habit of subdividing land between offspring reduced this still further. He therefore felt that the chief aim should be family planning; the government was indeed giving this high priority, and we had been surprised to see family planning posters high in the hills.

The porters felt uncomfortable in the unfamiliar surroundings of the farm school, and had left to find accommodation in the village. I felt much the same, but the children were so delighted to have the comfort of lights, beds, and a proper lavatory that we had accepted the invitation to stay, feeling strangely isolated from the everyday realities of a country where farms are not usually clean and straight-lined and orderly. The contrast was underlined by breakfast the next day at the Eveleys' house, comfortably furnished in western style, with the most enormous refrigerator I have ever seen, run on kerosene, and dainty flower-patterned cups, saucers, and plates. Everything in the house had been carried by porters from Pokhara, half a day's walk away; we accepted that westerners living abroad for any length of time felt the need for their accustomed home comforts, but could not help comparing the luxury there with the bare simplicity of the village houses, and wondering how it had been physically possible to carry the fridge over the hills.

Although we had appreciated the Eveleys' hospitality, we were glad to leave along a track which took us through several villages on a local trading route. Megan was frequently stopped by women who wanted to touch her hair and exclaimed at her soft pale skin. We had learnt the answers to half-understood questions, and I was able to tell them that she was a girl; she was five years old; yes, she was big for her age; and she had walked all the way, which we estimated at about 150 miles; that I was her mother, David her father, Jane a girl of eleven and Alistair a boy of ten. As we passed a group of women sitting on some steps in the sun, one of them swung Megan on to her knee, asking her if she would like to go home with her and be her daughter. Megan was alarmed at the friendly banter, and smiled shyly, but Jane and Alistair were always ready to talk and answered for her. Near the steps, the path opened into a wide sandy track high on a ridge, along which women were carrying heavy wooden planks for some new buildings. As they walked, the lengths of wood balanced on their shoulders (lengths which I would have expected two men to lift on a building site in England) swayed and threatened to topple them.

We were soon on a wide flat empty river bed, where it was hot under a cloudless, windless blue sky, the heat shimmering on the clay and sand of the paddy fields left dry after the last monsoon. On either side, the hills rose steeply, and to the north and east where we had walked in a figure of eight, we could still see the snow peaks of the Himalayas. At Suinkhet we found the squint-eyed minstrel sitting at a bench as if he had been waiting there for us. His mournful scraping accompanied us again for a while along the valley. The children and I could not resist taking off our shoes and socks to enjoy the coolness of the sandy mud. This horrified David, who was afraid we would catch some infection, and amused several Nepalese family groups making their way along the shimmering eternity of the river bed under the dazzling sun: although they were used to walking barefoot, they obviously expected foreigners to keep their shoes on.

The sprawling grassy track through Hyanja, where children and piglets were playing together, was shaken by the thudding whining sound of the only mechanical rice mill in the area. This had not been working when we had passed through the village before – it would have been impossible to be unaware of it, as the diesel-operated motor echoed for miles, the sound bouncing off the hills and vibrating from the ground. We stood in the doorway and watched as local farmers brought sacks of rice to be ground by machines which would not have looked out of place in the Science Museum in London.

A mule train had arrived just before us in the Tibetan camp, where we were again to spend the night. In the morning a few of the packs were opened, and some leisurely and good-natured bargaining transacted. Both buyers and sellers squatted round the open-necked sacks running the grains through their fingers to test the quality, and weighing it in level measuring jugs. Rice was sold in Pokhara for 15 rupees (60p) a pound, and by the end of the trail to Jomsom for double this amount. Fourteen of the men living at the camp were muleteers, and among the wealthiest people there.

7

Pokhara

The walk from the Tibetan camp back to Pokhara, which had felt such a very long way only a couple of weeks before, now seemed a mere morning stroll. At the top of the town, where a wide grassy square near a mission hospital marks the end of road traffic, we found a battered taxi. Into this we piled our luggage – rucksacks, porters' baskets, sleeping bags – and told the porters we would pay for them to be driven while we walked. They found this eccentric but acceptable, and we arranged to meet at the Yak Hotel in the centre of the town. The houses and shops lining the street as we walked slowly down to our rendezvous were the same we had passed on our way uphill at the start of the trek – but somehow now they looked less shabby and dilapidated.

The Yak Hotel was a plain square concrete block, three storeys high, on a corner in the middle of Pokhara. We were given two ground-floor rooms, each with two beds, for fifteen rupees a room, or sixty pence a night, regardless of how many of us there were. Both rooms were cold and dark, and the dusty concrete floor looked dirtier, colder, and harder than the beaten earth of the village houses, where we had usually been given mats on which to spread our sleeping bags. A small smelly cubicle next to our rooms provided a lavatory and shower – or rather a hole in the ground, a cold water tap, and a rusty tin can, with water from an uncovered and scummy outdoor tank.

Sonam was going to stay with us at the Yak for a night, to act as guide and interpreter for an exploratory trip the next day. We separated for the afternoon, which David and I spent with the children on a mild shopping spree, interrupted by visits to a sweet house opposite the hotel, where we sampled a variety of curried and sweet pastries, returning frequently for curried cones, *roshamgoola*, and

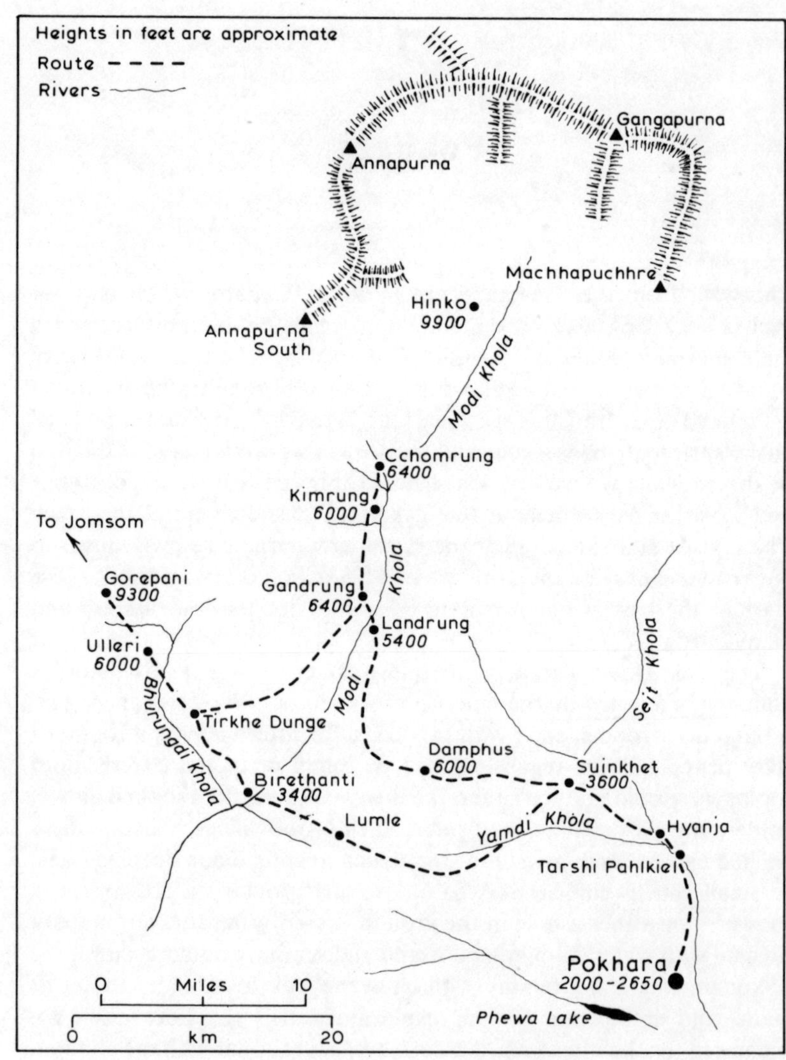

Our trekking route from Pokhara.

gulabjamen throughout the time we spent in Pokhara.

After the peace of the villages, Pokhara's main street seemed noisy and congested. Buffalo carts, battered brightly painted buses, and taxis which seemed to be falling apart and had to be push-started, narrowly avoided each other and pedestrians who wandered from one open-fronted shop to another or squatted to examine bangles, hair ribbons, fruit, vegetables, and spices displayed on the ground. As it grew dark, we watched from the hotel balcony while the traders collected their wares; candles and butter lamps twinkled in open windows or through the chinks of heavy wooden shutters under corrugated iron roofs held down by lumps of rock.

At dusk, the porters joined us for our last meal together, sitting awkwardly round the formica-topped table and ill at ease with the unfamiliar knives and forks. We could not persuade them to try anything other than their usual rice and dahl, but Megan was delighted to find she could have chicken hamburgers and fried bread. While we were waiting for our food, I made paper birds with flapping wings; each of the porters wanted one to take home. As a slightly more substantial parting gift, we presented each of them with one of our recorders, which they had sneaked out to play whenever they thought we were not listening. We knew they coveted our parkas, but we explained that we needed these for the rest of our stay; they seemed touched by the recorders, and delighted when we shared our last few bars of chocolate between them.

We discovered early the next morning that the hotel was very conveniently placed at the starting point for taxis and buses, which began touting for custom soon after 6 a.m., with much hooting and shouting from attendant boys hoping to earn a few pice. Even without the street noises, we could not have been able to sleep much after six, as the wood for the hotel kitchen, for some reason placed on the flat roof, was stacked outside our bedroom before being carried up. The stacking method was simple: log after log was hurled from an outside woodpile on to the heap, each log bouncing off our wall.

At the Tibetan camp, Sonam had managed to find out where the Khambas who had recently been rounded up and brought south from Mustang had been taken, and we had decided to try to find their camp. He told us that he was himself a Khamba, although neither he nor his family had been involved in any raiding activities. He was half eager, half afraid, at the thought of searching them out, but offered to show us the way.

We had first to take a bus for an hour. At the airport, which was also the bus station, we bumped into Curly Bill and Solti, who were waiting for the plane from Kathmandu in the hope of finding another portering job. Peter had already started the long walk home to his family. As the bus seemed unlikely to leave for some time, we sat together at one of the shanty shacks we had avoided two weeks earlier, enjoying a glass of tea and some hotly curried fried dahl sold in packets like salted peanuts. Suddenly Sonam leapt up, shouting, "Quick – the bus is crying!" This amused the children so much that it has become a family catchphrase, most unfairly as it was almost the only mistake in idiomatic English he made.

It would have taken a couple of days on the same bus to reach the Indian border. We climbed steadily, rattling and jumping along the steeply twisting road with frequent loud prolonged hooting, views of valleys and mountains opening up at each turn only to be obliterated again by the next. Several partially cleared landslides set the road surface on a jolting slant.

We climbed down with relief from the overcrowded bus at a small roadside village in a valley, beside a bridge over a low river. Three Tibetans got off at the same stop. To Sonam's alarm, a fully armed uniformed soldier was standing guard at the bridge, positioned at the foot of the path we were to take, obviously to stop unauthorized persons such as ourselves from passing. We were afraid this might be the end of our search, and sat at the village bus stop café to drink a glass of tea and work out our tactics. Sonam was obviously torn between curiosity, the duty he felt to protect us, and apprehension; we suggested he should wait at the café for us, but after some thought he said he would come some of the way, provided we could pass the soldier.

This we did surprisingly easily, by merely walking very fast past him in a group, talking together and totally ignoring his presence. He was very young, and looked uncertain what he should do about us, as he was presumably only expecting to have to challenge his own people. When we glanced back a little later, he was still looking in our direction with a puzzled expression. It was a stiff two and a half hour climb up two or three thousand feet, on brilliant orange-red soil, past a few scattered houses where the people looked at us suspiciously and did not return our greeting. At last we saw the camp from a high ridge, hidden in a bowl in the hills. There was no sign of any other houses, and the site had been well chosen for its seclusion, as no one not intending to go there would be likely to stumble across it.

Sonam was still with us as we walked down to a cluster of dilapidated but once elegant old houses, tents and shacks. We were immediately challenged and taken to the camp administrator, who was not sure whether to welcome us or turn us away. Chairs were brought out for us to sit on, cigarettes and suspicious civilities exchanged. The usual hospitable glass of tea was however not offered, to our regret. For some time, we sat in an awkward group, chatting generally with the camp administrator, who was delighted to practise his fluent stilted English and have company from outside the camp's claustrophobic and confining limits. A sad skinny little man in a green suit, he came from Kathmandu, had been sent to take charge only four days earlier, and thoroughly disliked his new appointment. He had no idea how long he would be there, and little knowledge about the duties of his isolated post.

Gradually, the conversation worked round to the reason for our sudden and unexpected appearance. The camp administrator turned frequently to confer with a burly and determined watchdog, the chief of police for the camp, who was far from pleased to see us and kept, as Sonam told us later, telling his companion to say nothing. To our alarm, Sonam was taken aside and questioned closely, reluctantly giving details of his family and origins. A dozen young policemen sprawled on the grass, playing cards but obviously listening intently.

We asked if we might look round. The chief of police and the administrator did not wish to appear unfriendly or inhospitable, but had after all their duty to perform, and only agreed to take us on a conducted tour after much discussion and after we had promised not to take photos. "We will show you everything systematically," they promised, warning us not to ask questons.

The village had once been a prosperous Chetri settlement, the centre of the area, but the two-storey homes of the village leaders were in a state of neglect and disrepair. We were ushered down to a row of semi-ruins being used as meagre shops, and were immediately surrounded by a curious crowd, jostling to talk to us. This was actively discouraged as we were hustled on, past the houses to a wide flat grassy space where several long mat prefabs and tents had been erected as temporary accommodation. One of the tents, more imposing than the others, long, white, with an elegant black border and design, was the lama's. For a minute or two, we were allowed to stop and talk with two of the Khamba men. They told us they did not want to be there but were not allowed to leave; and that the Nepalese government provided one doctor and food for the men, but none for the women and children. The police chief and administrator began to shift uncomfortably, and soon hurried us away firmly.

"The Nepalese government is sympathetic. Arrangements will be made for schooling and other things," the administrator assured us. Again we were told we must not ask questions, and questions must not be answered. We should have made official arrangements for our visit through the Chief of Police in Pokhara, and not have visited the camp without his permission – which we were certain would not have been granted. "In Nepal, you must always see the Chief of Police; he can tell you where to go and where not to go. This is a restricted area; I do not know why, I am under government orders." The camp's police chief looked severely disapproving while even this limited information was given, but the administrator went on to admit that the people could not come and go freely from the camp. They could, however, apply for day passes and this had been the case with the three men who had travelled from Pokhara on the bus.

All the people we saw at the camp were well dressed, in the traditional Tibetan costume which looks so much warmer than that of Nepali villagers. Conditions seemed no worse than in many villages, and better than in some. There were a few horses. The people looked healthy and strong, but seemed, we thought, frustrated by their enforced idleness, with no work to occupy their minds and time, as well as by the restriction of their freedom.

Our tour was brought to an abrupt end when we again tried to talk to some of the English-speaking men of the camp. We were escorted some way up the slope, and took our leave with mutual apologies: from us for causing embarrassment, which we obviously had: and from the administrator for not allowing us to take photos or talk freely with the Khambas. "It will be better for you to go to one of the established Tibetan camps near Pokhara; there you can see the people settled and admire their handicrafts," he advised us as we left.

Sonam was eager to return to his family, and worried that they might suffer some sort of repercussion after his interrogation at the camp, so left us as soon as we reached Pokhara. We were relieved when David met him a few weeks later and he had heard nothing about the unofficial visit to his tribesmen.

We still had one day to spend in Pokhara before returning to Kathmandu, and planned some leisurely sight-seeing and shopping. After an unintentionally early breakfast – the crying of the buses in front of the hotel and the noisy stacking of wood against our door had again woken us at dawn – we went to look at what was left of the Phewa dam. Not long after the auspicious occasion (a favourite Nepalese description) of its opening, it had unceremoniously collapsed, leaving the town again without electricity as it always had been. A third of the structure had completely disintegrated, and most of the water it had held back had drained away, leaving the Phewa river bed empty except for a stagnant pool where some women were doing their washing and a few buffalo were drinking. A solitary bulldozer was at work. The reason for the dam's collapse was not known, but it was rumoured that it had been caused by faulty concrete. Indian aid had supplied the funds, and the unproven suspicion was that good materials had been supplied but misappropriated. Many people we spoke to in Pokhara were resentful of the expense of the coronation, feeling that the money would have been better spent repairing the damage, a task which was likely to take several years.

The Phewa dam was one of only a few in the whole country. Others supplied power for the Kathmandu valley towns and several towns in the Terai, and one or two villages in the north near the Tibetan border. Most of the people in the villages are still, as they will no doubt continue to do, relying on little butter lamps, candles, or the occasional luxury of a hurricane or tilley lamp for light.

The rivers tumble and rush down the mountains, their water power wasted because of the enormous technical and financial problems of harnessing its potential. Electricity, unlikely to be available to most villages in the near future, would, I feel sure, revolutionize life in the best possible way. For heat, light, and cooking, the people would no longer have to rely on the diminishing natural resources of the woods, forests, and scrub. The problem of erosion could be dealt with, and children would be more likely to be able to attend school regularly if their traditional chore of woodcutting was removed. The accident and even mortality rate, especially among infants, through falling or crawling into floor-level wood fires, would drop. Already, in the short time the Phewa dam was in operation, the standard and conditions of living in Pokhara had improved enormously – hence the dismay at the dam's collapse, and anger that it could not be rebuilt immediately.

Because of Pokhara's attractive river and lake, and its accessibility from Kathmandu by both road and air, a rash of tourist hotels and guest houses had sprung up, with names like Mountain or Lake View, Joe's Place, and even Hotel Lonely. To own a holiday home in Pokhara was also something of a Nepalese status symbol, especially if it was built in that most esteemed material, concrete. The royal family's concrete summer residence looked more like a small military prison, although a large grey house belonging to the queen mother and a royal picnic chalet on stilts were slightly more attractive.

The royal family also owned one of the few attractive modern buildings I saw in Nepal, a luxurious hotel called the Fishtail Lodge and combining functional simplicity with elegant suitability to its surroundings. Unfortunately this and the shabbier humbler guest houses had lost their chief tourist attraction when the dam burst and the water drained out of the Phewa Lake and river. Beside the causeway approach to the double octagon of the Fishtail Lodge we watched a group of women working with the concentration of bees whose hive has been destroyed to build a dam intended to keep the remaining water in the lake – a long slow task of fetching earth in baskets which seemed unlikely to succeed.

The hotel had been open for about eight years, and run for most of this time by one Fred Barker who, after making Nepal his home for many years, had suddenly been refused a visa extension. It was rumoured that this was because of interest in and possibly involvement with the Khambas. After a disastrous period under a new manager, a member of the influential Rana family had taken over a few days before we arrived in Pokhara. Ujjal Rana had previously worked in one of the big Kathmandu hotels (also owned by the royal family), and gave an impression of suave courteous efficiency which, as the Fishtail had not yet reopened, we could not put to the test.

We asked him where the hotel's water supply came from, and where the effluent went – in both cases, the answer was the lake. He in turn asked our advice about how to develop boating facilities on the lake, where the king's power boat, housed in a substantial two-storey building, was the only boat allowed apart from a few traditional solid canoes. Two boys who looked about ten but were much older persuaded us, without much difficulty, that we should not miss the opportunity of a trip in their canoes which looked efficient enough although clumsy, each about ten feet long hollowed out of a single tree trunk. "Boat trees are very expensive," the boys told us, charging us five rupees (20p) an hour for each boat, which included a boy to row with a flat wooden paddle. They took us to a little temple in a treed courtyard on what used to be an island, but could with the low water level be equally easily reached on foot along a causeway. Variegated doves and pigeons were roosting and cooing in the trees and on the pagoda roof, not at all dismayed by the sight of a boy with a bag full of live pigeons. Two grand carved lions stood guard at the corners of the temple courtyard.

Back at the Yak Hotel, in the first-floor dining room, a spartan contrast to the Fishtail's elegance, David and I had ordered our usual dahlbat, and the children were debating the relative merits of hamburgers and chips or omelettes and chips, to be followed by tinned pineapple, when there was a low rumbling sound and the floor started to vibrate gently under our feet. We had been told that the hotel would soon have a generator installed, and at first imagined that this was being tested. The rumbling grew stronger, as if all the buses were revving up at once in the street, then the whole building began to shake and the candle flames flickered uncertainly. There was a crash from the roof as the cook dropped a pile of plates and all the Nepali hotel staff and guests who had been standing poised and apprehensive shot like scalded cats down the stairs and into the street. They were closely followed by our children, who said later, "We didn't know what it was, but if they thought they ought to get out, so did we."

By this time, David and I realized we were experiencing an earthquake, but, perhaps foolishly, stayed in the building, and went on to the balcony to look into the street. Below us, people were running around shouting and pointing up at the hotel, one of the tallest most substantial constructions in the area. It was shaking visibly. I picked out an open space a little way up the road to run out of the way of falling masonry, if it should be necessary. And then it was all over. The whole experience, which left my legs trembling, had taken no more than a minute.

The conversation for the next hour was all of earthquakes, which occur fairly frequently in Pokhara and the surrounding district. A long very deep crack only a few feet wide runs the length of the town behind the village street, but it is many years since there was a tremor violent enough to cause serious damage or open up any sizeable new fissures.

The earthquake was followed by a spectacular thunderstorm. For seconds at a time, the sky was bright with a strange white light, the clouds alternately back lit by sheet lightning and then obscured by torrential rain. By morning, the air was clear and the mountains showed up sharply, the snow line considerably lower than usual.

8

In the Kathmandu Valley

After staying in village houses, our arrival at the Waterhouses' elegant residence on a ridge overlooking the capital came as something of a cultural shock – particularly as we turned up in the middle of a British Council farewell lunch for the Allegri String Quartet. David Waterhouse, the British Council's man in Kathmandu, had arranged for the quartet to play for an audience of privileged foreigners and the Nepalese cultural élite, and for the children at the British primary school. As the official representative of British culture in Nepal, he also had somewhat less esoteric duties to perform than arranging for western musical delights, such as keeping a fatherly eye on young people engaged in VSO activities, arranging language courses and supervising their work in schools and hospitals, and occasionally helping British tourists with problems such as lost passports.

There was a tightly knit embassy group in Kathmandu, as in most capital cities, and although David and Verena insisted they were nothing to do with the British Embassy, they were nevertheless involved with its inevitable social life. The British were the first people to have a resident, later elevated to ambassador, in Kathmandu, and during the Rana regime Britain's official representative was one of the few foreigners tolerated in the country. After the overthrow of the Ranas and the opening of Nepal's borders in 1950, the British Council established itself alongside the embassy, and a couple of dozen countries installed embassies and consulates. As the Nepalese have a talent for maintaining complete neutrality, while playing off nation against nation when it comes to financial aid, various development schemes have been financed by the Americans, British, Swiss, Germans, Chinese, Indians and Russians.

A few days after our return to Kathmandu, Russian culture had its

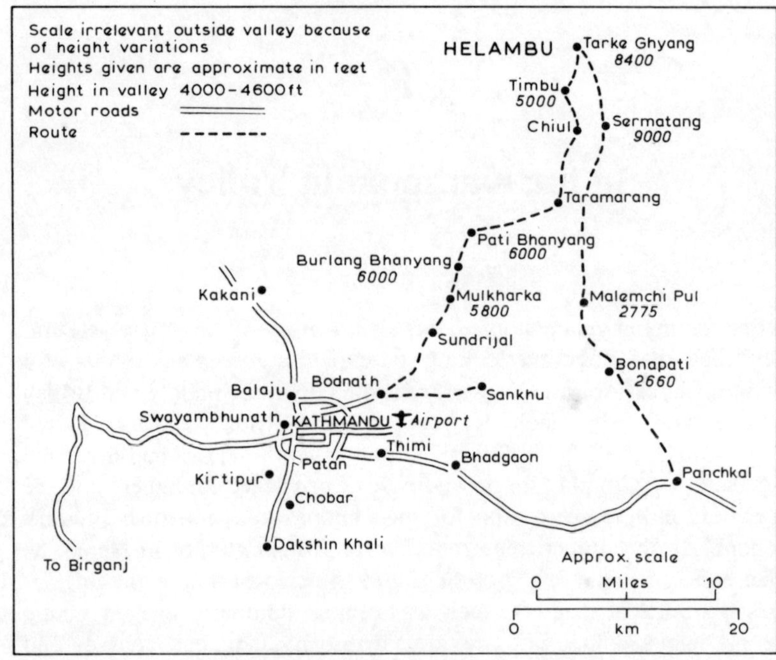

Kathmandu Valley and Helambu trek.

turn, with a visit by the Bolshoi Ballet. The last thing I had expected to do in Nepal was see the Bolshoi Ballet, but I was beginning to feel that I had stepped into Alice's Wonderland, where anything could happen and often did, and nothing seemed extraordinary. The theatre was packed to overspill, with extra places created by using the steps of the steeply tiered rows as seats. Most of the foreigners we had already met at the Waterhouses' and the Nepalese friends of the Giris we had met while staying with them seemed to be there, and we exchanged nods and namastes with acquaintances as we pushed our way to our seats; the theatre was obviously the place to see and be seen by all the right people. Each separate item was introduced by a long and involved explanation given first in Nepali and then all over again in English, and was then danced to taped music. At one point, the tape broke, but the dancers continued as if nothing had happened.

As well as official foreign representation and cultural exchange, there were any number of unofficial friendship societies in the capital. We even saw a sign on a door stating in English that it was the entrance to a Nepalese-Korean meeting place, and ourselves attended one stilted semi-formal meeting of the English Nepalese Society, where everyone was very careful not to say anything which might offend anyone else. A wealthy Rana told us about the elaborate arrangements for his daughter's traditional no-expense-spared wedding, with interested smiles and polite approving nods from his listeners of both nationalities. A Nepalese chamber of commerce official talked solemnly and at length about the great progress made in Nepalese trade and business – more polite agreement.

Britain was represented only by ourselves, David and Verena, and the Scotts. Michael Scott, British Ambassador at the time, and a perfect example of the urbane FO social ideal, kept insisting that there had been "no unnecessary expense" for the coronation, and that everything in Nepal was lovely. His wife, an immaculately groomed and beautifully dressed American lady, was having a busy time, as she was to be hostess at a British Embassy garden party for British VIP guests and residents. As royalty was to be present in the form of Prince Charles, Earl Mountbatten of Burma, and the Duke and Duchess of Gloucester, it was very important for mere commoners to know how to behave, and Jennifer Scott had gathered all the British wives together to instruct them in the art of curtseying.

As well as the official embassy in Kathmandu, the British maintain a holiday residence fourteen miles from the city along a mountainous hairpin-bend road at Kakani. David and Verena took us there one day with a picnic prepared from the leftovers of the Allegri String Quartet's lunch party; we ate on a verandah supported by pretentious white pillars, with an uninterrupted view across a deep valley to the North Western Himalaya. Huge old-fashioned picnic hampers seemed entirely in keeping with the colonial style of the ambassadorial retreat, a long bungalow under a red-painted corrugated iron roof; privacy was ensured by a high wire-mesh fence enclosing an area of rolling down-like grass.

It is expected that foreign officials maintain a life style appropriate to their position as representatives of their country abroard, and David and Verena were no exception to the unwritten rule that anyone wishing to be respected in Nepal must have a number of servants.

Directly or indirectly, they were supporting a dozen or more people. There was Ram, homely, comfortable, and plump, who came in every day to look after the three children, often staying until they were all in bed, devoted to and adored by them, like the very best sort of old-fashioned English nanny.

Then there was Krishna, a handsome young man, always cheerful even when suffering from a bad boil which eventually made him feel so ill that he did not appear for work for several days. Krishna had a wife and several children, and another on the way although he seemed very vague about when it was due, all living in a little two-storey house on a dusty valley track a few miles outside the town. He was the cook; apparently unflappable, he catered equally happily for large official gatherings or for any number of children and friends, discussing each day's menu with Verena.

The first person we usually saw in the morning was Tashi, a tiny wizened irrepressible Tibetan who silently served breakfast, with an almost permanent grin which only occasionally vanished, leaving him looking sad like an out-of-work clown. Tashi turned up on time every day of the year except for feast days and festivals, when he didn't turn up at all, sometimes for several days, until his hangover had gone. After dark, a *chokidar*, or nightwatchman, whom I never heard speak but who appeared smiling to open the gate, was on duty, sitting in a little outside room beside the garage all night. A couple of gardeners put in sporadic appearances; every morning, a silent middle-aged-looking young man swept the floors, and twice a week the dhobi called for the laundry.

The children and I found it difficult to get used to having so many people doing things for us, and I fought a silent battle of pride with Ram, who had a genius for finding our dirty clothes and removing them before I had had a chance to wash them, returning them neatly folded and dry the same evening. The Nepalese winter sun was strong and hot for several hours each day, although the mornings were often cold and foggy, the fog rarely lifting completely before mid morning, and at night the temperature dropped to near freezing. The swift sunsets were brilliant and exciting, as we had an uninterrupted view of the mountains in the distance across the panorama of the city. During the monsoon months, this view would be obscured by rain clouds and the daytime temperature would reach the 90s, with several hours of rain each day cooling the air and bringing night temperatures as low as 60°F.

David was by this time involved with filming, and we rarely saw him as he had moved with the film crew into a little house behind the Soaltee Oberoi, a large and impressive modern hotel belonging to the royal family. The rest of us soon settled into a routine in Kathmandu, using the cold early morning hours to keep up with the children's school work and setting out on foot as soon as the sun tempted us away from this chore to explore the valley. The three principal towns of the valley, Kathmandu, Patan, and Bhadgaon, and the valley villages are a tourists' paradise, with more temples to the square mile than anywhere else in the world.

All this ancient exotic beauty was created by the Newari people who lived in the valley long before the beginning of any accurate historical records. No one knows where they came from, or when: some say from India, some say Tibet; some claim they have been in the valley since prehistoric times, others since the sixth century BC. What is quite certain is that by the time the Hindu Malla kings brought their faith and caste system from India, in the middle ages, the Newaris were well established in the valley, with a sophisticated Buddhist culture; and that for several hundred years under royal Malla patronage their art enjoyed a golden age. Towards the end of the Malla era, each of the valley towns was a separate kingdom, ruled by an independent Malla king; these kings competed in the collection of buildings, pictures, and sculptures, rather than politically and militarily. Although the division of the valley into separate kingdoms made it easier for the Shahs of Gorkha to defeat the Mallas in the mid eighteenth century, it also left a heritage of beauty created by the Newaris and financed by the Mallas.

There are about half a million Newaris in Nepal, and half of them still live in the valley towns which they created. They are Buddhist and Hindu – or a mixture of both – in about equal numbers, and have adopted the Hindu caste system so enthusiastically that even Buddhist priests have their place on the caste ladder, nearly at the top but slightly less elevated socially than the Newari Deo Brahman caste of Hindu family priests (who, to add to the complications of trying to understand Nepalese tribes and castes, are not necessarily the same as the Brahman people on the top rung of the national caste ladder).

In spite of the theoretical equality of all people announced by the king, the two dozen or so Newari castes are still aware of their traditional position. At the bottom of the caste ladder are the Halhulu, road sweepers, and between them and the priests are a couple of dozen divisions, such as Bare goldsmiths nearly at the top, merchants and craftsmen of the Uray caste, Jogi musicians and tailors, and Jyapu farming people, with their distinctive black saris bordered in red and worn differently from saris of other people. The Jyapu are the only Newaris to bury rather than cremate their dead, presumably because as farmers land is easily available – most other Newaris are town dwellers or live in villages of terraced houses with few open spaces.

Many ancient customs governing Newari life have been retained, such as the symbolic marriage between a young girl and a tree: as this marriage cannot be dissolved, she always has the status of a married woman, and divorce is simple. Some Newari festivals have been adopted nationally, like Gai Jatra, the festival of sacred cows, when the streets are filled with people dressed as cows to help the dead into heaven. To share the financial burden of civic and religious responsibilities, the Newaris long ago worked out a system of *guthi*, clubs and co-operatives – *digu puja guthi* to pay for festivals, feasts, and pujas; general guthi with joint land ownership to take charge of road and bridge repairs, temple maintenance, and funeral and cremation costs; and voluntary social club guthi.

In Patan, sometimes known as Lalitpur, one of the ancient Newari cities which was once a separate kingdom but now almost merges with Kathmandu, many Newari people still live in the old *bahal* or Buddhist courtyards. Originally built as a monastic community, a bahal includes a temple or shrine and a collection of tall narrow terraced houses round a central open courtyard, and later Hindu housing was often built in much the same style, the courtyard then being known as a *chok*.

One of the oldest and most respected of the Buddhist courtyard communities in Patan is Oku Bahal. Two thousand Newaris live in Oku Bahal, most of them members of the gold and silversmith Bare caste and involved in the ancient art of casting or other high-class metal work. David Waterhouse wanted to buy an Indra figure by one of Patan's leading sculptors, Bodi Raj Sakya, who lived in Oku Bahal;

I went with him to see the sculptor at work. We found him in his studio on the top floor of a tall thin wedge of a house with a view over rooftops. Several figures of Indra, king of the gods and god of rain, littered the floor in various stages. Each one took him, he told us, about a week to complete; working on several at once he could complete a dozen a week, selling them to a shop for around £35 and earning more than most people in Nepal could ever hope to. Tourists might have to pay anything up to £70 for one of his larger figures, depending on their nationality and the state of trade.

Sakya is the surname of members of the Newari Bare gold and silversmith caste, many of whom are closely and most at least distantly related. Bodi Raj Sakya's father before him, and his brother, were both sculptors, all three working in the painstaking traditional "lost wax" technique. By this method, although each figure looks identical, the same mould is never used twice. A model of the figure is first made in soft dark-coloured wax, a mixture of beeswax, ghee, and resin, kept pliable over a brazier. It has to be perfect in every detail, even the tiniest delicately bent finger, before it can be coated with clay in the next stage of the operation. By the time it has been covered in several layers first of fine grey clay and then of coarse rough clay mixed with husks, it is an ugly mis-shapen object.

When the clay is quite dry, the model is heated and the wax is poured out so that it can be used again, and casting can begin. The metal – it may be copper, brass, bronze, iron, or even silver – is melted a little at a time in an open crucible in a closed kiln. In a second kiln the clay mould is heated and then taken out and supported upside down on bricks ready to receive the liquid metal. When the mould is full it is left to cool for a little while, cold water is poured over it, and it is then plunged into cold water. As soon as it is cool enough to touch, the clay mould is broken, but still the process is not finished. The figure must be sandpapered smooth, engraved with delicate lines, and perhaps have jewels set into it. Jewelled nipples are popular.

Although each figure made in this way is an individual work of art, and far more prized and more costly than the mass-produced figures now being made for the tourist market, there is little scope for originality. The artist's inspiration is almost entirely religious, but with such a multitude of deities to choose from there is plenty of variety although traditional details are closely copied.

Coppersmiths belong to a lower caste, and live in a separate equally tightly knit community in Patan. The children and I wandered one day into the copper workers' area, where the noise was deafening and conversation impossible. In every house, and in front of the houses, copper pots were being beaten into traditional shapes over braziers. A twelve-year-old schoolboy, who spoke rapid pidgin-type English and told us that he also spoke several other languages, attached himself to us as an unofficial but enthusiastic guide, and soon persuaded us to leave the banging and clanging of the copper-working streets for the comparative peace of the woodworking area, where his relatives lived and worked.

Many of the houses he led us past had impressive elaborate carving round the doors and windows, and even whole panels devoted to intricate formal designs of birds and animals. Although much of the carving was dirty and neglected, some was being cleaned and restored in the general frenzy of pre-coronation repairs. Behind the houses of a long narrow street carpenters were busy making new door and window frames and roof struts. We were escorted up wooden open-tread stairs and through low doorways into low dark-ceilinged rooms to be tempted by the work of our young guide's relatives. Turned wooden bowls encrusted with gilt medallions and carved figures, both ancient and modern, were brought out for us to admire, with a wealth of bewildering mythological detail.

Ironically, it is the tourist industry, combined with the demand of devout Buddhist refugees from Tibet, which have revived religious art and the allied crafts in Nepal – and as Nepalese art is always based on religious mythology, in however unbelieving a way it may find itself into the luggage of tourists, this has brought about both a new awareness of the commercial value of the country's heritage and with it a general artistic revival, after a couple of centuries during which neither the Shahs nor the Ranas did much to encourage creativity. At the same time, it has however resulted in the mass production of second-rate souvenirs, which are all too often made of inferior materials and poorly finished. Many tourists either cannot tell the difference or cannot afford the better-quality items. Although there is an official ban on the removal from the country of antique works of art, this ban is often ignored by both buyer and seller and there is a flourishing trade in antiques; so the more discriminating visitors help unintentionally in the gradual depletion of the country's stock of ancient works of art and in their replacement by inferior modern copies.

One craft which has been less affected by tourism, and which is gradually declining because of the introduction of materials such as plastic, is pottery, the occupation of the Newari Kuma people. As an amateur potter, I wanted to find out about the techniques which produced the traditional pots and stylized elephant-shaped plant holders sold from great precarious heaps in one of the Kathmandu bazaar squares, and persuaded Krishna to come with me as interpreter to the pottery village of Thimi a few miles outside the city. All along Thimi's main street, pots were stacked outside open-fronted shops; a van was being loaded with pots for the bazaar, and several men staggered past us bowlegged under the weight of huge water pots slung from yokes across their shoulders. Narrow alleys led past high gates opening through walls into backyard potteries, and in the side streets and squares there was just room to walk between rows of pots drying in the sun or waiting to be fired.

The square open area at a small crossroads was almost completely blocked by a kiln – a great smoking mound of pots and straw covered with sand, with rows of holes to allow the steam and smoke to escape. More elaborate permanent kilns are built of brick, and packed with up to a thousand pots at a time; straw is packed round and over the pots, with a layer of clay to keep the heat in. I asked about the firing temperature: "*tato*" – hot – I was told, and when I pressed for greater precision this rose to "*dere tato*" – very hot.

We were invited into a family pottery by a man who had started work as an apprentice potter at the age of twelve. All his male relations were potters, and a group of small boys who followed us around would probably also become potters, although it was apparently not considered a suitable occupation for women. The potter demonstrated his technique for my benefit, kneading fine sand into the clay before throwing on a wheel, an old lorry tyre, set close to the ground so that he could work from a squatting position, spinning it into motion with a wooden paddle. As the pot grew from a hump of buff-coloured clay to a tall water pot he gradually rose until he was standing over it, legs flexed apart, one arm thrust inside it almost up to the shoulder as he checked its thickness and smoothness. He worked swiftly with an economy of time and effort which I envied, tidying the base of each pot before removing it from the wheel so that there would be no need for time-consuming trimming and turning later. Even the formal stylized elephants I had admired in the Kathmandu bazaar were made from a collection of thrown shapes.

None of the pots was glazed, the only colour an occasional band of thick darker slip painted on roughly or a burnishing of black from the ashes of the firing. From throwing a pot to unpacking the kiln, we were told the process took about three days – a day for drying in the sun, another day for firing, and a day for the kiln to cool. The finished pots, having been fired only once to a rather uncertain temperature, were brittle and often porous, but cheap, and the traditional shapes simple, functional, and unconsciously elegant.

Clay found in the valley was used both by the potters and for brickmaking, which, because of the monsoon, was a seasonal occupation, the paddy fields producing rice in the wet summer months and bricks in the winter. As it was the brick season, many of the valley paddy fields between Kathmandu and Thimi, and further on towards Bhadgaon, had a semi-urban appearance, with family groups busy digging the clay from trenches, roughly banging and rolling it into huge wedges, then shaping the bricks at great speed. Both men and women wore traditional costume, the men working in their long white shirts like old-fashioned nightshirts and tight-calved baggy-bottomed white cotton jodhpurs and the women in long wrap-around skirts or half saris, often with a baby or older child strapped to their backs. The first bricks of the season had been used to build or repair kilns scattered across the landscape like tall narrow windowless houses.

Many houses are still built with cheap unfired bricks which have mellowed to a warm soft brown, but are liable to be washed away by the monsoon rains. The art of making the sort of bricks used under the Malla kings was more sophisticated, and had been forgotten until John Sanday, an Englishman in charge of the restoration of the Hanuman Dhoka, rediscovered it. He wanted to match the old so-called *telia* glazed bricks. The glaze brought out the colours of the clay, and as telia means "oiled" it was thought that oil had been used in the process. After several messy experiments, John Sanday discovered that this was not the case, and eventually worked out a way to make bricks almost exactly matching the old ones under laboratory tests – a long and complicated process, which no doubt explains why it was discontinued. The clay had to come from a special seam, be cleaned and made workable by trampling, and the glaze, made from slurry from clay found in a village called Hedegaon just outside Kathmandu, applied to the unfired bricks, after maturing for at least six years under straw to allow the monsoon rains to create a sort of colouring fungus growth.

Gradually the chaos of restoration work was being sorted out, not only round the Hanuman Dhoka but also in the other valley towns. The children and I walked through Thimi to the eighth-century Malla city of Bhadgaon (or Bhaktapur – both names are used) one day, arriving just as the newly relaid Durbar Square was being washed. The aid of Nepal's noble fire brigade had been enlisted, and several soldiers in uniform were enthusiastically directing water from an ancient hosepipe more or less indiscriminately at the street, buildings, and passers-by. Almost as much water was escaping from holes along the entire length of the hose as from the nozzle. The effect was bizarre, with the uniformed soldiers, the antique fire engine, and the jets of water and spray from the holes, as if a row of invisible whales lying close together were all blowing at once. Women in saris and men in official white costume ducked and slid under the erratic arches of the jet, and the glistening curves of the water turned into miniature rainbows in the strong sunlight against the surrounding elegant carved, repainted, regilded buildings.

The most impressive of these was an old Malla palace, now a museum, where we took refuge from the water and were shown the exhibits by a young guide who spoke good English but knew very little history. Surprisingly modern-looking rice paintings, many reputedly hundreds of years old, showed semi-historical, semi-mythical scenes in rich glowing colours. Stone god figures, many with split personalities, half one god, half another, some half-male, half-female, referred to incidents in the confusingly active life of the Hindu deities. One of the Malla kings was himself an accomplished artist and scholar, and decorated one long wall of his bedchamber with friezes. From the deep windows lining the opposite wall, overlooking the Durbar Square, we were almost at eye level with a gilded statue of the Malla king Bhupatendra, gloriously aloof on a tall pillar under a golden parasol.

As we wandered downhill from the Durbar Square area, through narrow medieval streets of shops half under cover, the children were alarmed to find themselves face to face with an enormous white bull which looked as if it had escaped from a cave painting. It was enjoying its sacred right to wander freely in the streets, and in spite of its powerful shoulders and massive head was as gentle as a lamb. We saw it first ambling from shop to shop, and later lying peacefully in the middle of the road. Pedestrians carrying baskets of vegetables or hardware slung on yokes sidestepped patiently round the gigantic slumbering male fertility symbol.

Instead of walking the eight miles back, as we had come, through Thimi and past the brick fields, we joined a bus queue near a walled market just outside the city's tall ornate arched gateway. The bus turned out to be an old ambulance, which left only when every seat was at least doubly occupied, every corner crammed, and five people had somehow managed to squeeze in front with the driver. As we bumped and rattled along a new Chinese road, past an area devoted to modern brick works, we talked to a waiter from the Soaltee Oberoi whose ambition was to work in a hotel in America. Just outside the city, we passed a large rectangular artificial pool, and asked him why no one was using it as a washing place, as it was unusual to find an expanse of water without a group of women washing their clothes or hair in it. He told us that Sidhi Pokhari, as it is called, is cursed.

Once upon a time, a wicked *naga*, or snake, who lived in Sidhi Pokhari, used to draw people to their deaths in its waters by making them think there was gold floating on its surface. A holy man from Thimi decided he could outwit the naga with the help of a friend, and plunged into the water. If milk came to the surface, the friend would know he had been killed; but if blood appeared on the surface, it would mean that the snake had been overcome, and holy rice must be thrown over the victor as he emerged. Obviously, the holy man had to take on the form of a snake himself to fight the naga, and the rice was essential to reverse the transformation.

Although the wicked naga lost the battle, the holy man is presumably still living in the pool as a snake, since his companion was so terrified when he saw blood rising to the surface that he ran home to Thimi forgetting all about the holy rice. So although Sidhi Pokhari, which is 500 years old, is quite big enough to be used as a swimming pool, no one dares to bathe in its water.

9

Valley Gods and Temples

It is impossible to walk far in the valley without coming across a temple and being aware of the role of religion in everyday life. The temples may be elaborate many storeyed golden roofed pagodas, small wood or brick buildings with ornate carving, strange white dome-shaped *stupas* or *chaityas* of varying sizes, or tiny shrines sheltering a single statue. The gods, whose worship is both a day-to-day affair and the excuse for countless complex festivals, are so numerous that no one seems to know exactly how many there are supposed to be.

In the beginning, however, there was God: this, in spite of the multiplicity of individual gods, is the underlying belief of both the Hindu and Buddhist faiths. Way, way back in the dim distant unrecorded past, the spirit of God existed everywhere, in men and beasts, animate and inanimate objects. Early animistic beliefs are still present in Nepal's present mixture of creeds, much as Christian worship in the West includes earlier pagan elements, but with one great difference: whereas Christianity has sought to eliminate other faiths, claiming to be the only true faith, the Nepalese have with a tolerance which is their greatest virtue been quite happy to enlarge their belief to embrace other explanations.

Although it seems strange at first that both Hindus and Buddhists often worship at the same temple, not worried about the distinction between creeds which is so important to, say, Christians and Muslims or Catholics and Protestants, it never strikes the Nepalese as odd. God was in the beginning, and what came after God can be equally well explained by a number of gods, each representing one part of the universal spirit, or by following the code of men sent from God who have attained such spiritual greatness as to become one with God.

Nepal's history has often been violent and bloody, but there has never been a battle over religion. "One God or many gods: it's the same thing, just expressed in different ways. Why should one of us wish to change the way of the other?" a Nepalese friend asked me one day when we were discussing the differences and similarities between Hindu, Buddhist, and Christian beliefs. In Nepal, everyone is, and always has been, free to worship as he pleases – but to attempt to convert someone of one faith to another is forbidden. Christians who have preached conversion have, quite recently, been imprisoned, their intolerance breeding in its turn intolerance.

The Hindu faith, which is far older than Christianity, favours a multiplicity of gods, through whom the Universal Reality, the Absolute Spirit (God) is expressed in different ways. In a picturesque trinity above all other gods, many of whom are in any case their manifestations under a variety of names or their offspring, are Brahma, the Creator, Vishnu, the Preserver, and Shiva, Destroyer and Regenerator. Brahma himself, it is said, divided the occupants of the world into four groups, creating the caste system. As woman issued forth from Adam's rib in Jewish and Christian mythology, the four Hindu castes sprang from different parts of Brahma's body: Brahmans, the highest caste, traditionally priests, came from his head and took his holy name; the rulers and fighters, Kshatriyas (Chetri) are below the Brahmans, coming from his arm; inferior to both, created from his leg, are the merchants and traders of the Vaisya caste, and the lowest of the low, servants and labourers, from his foot, are the Sudras. The numerous subdivisions of these four castes cannot be attributed directly to Brahma, whose task finished with creation, and who is rarely mentioned and even more rarely worshipped now in Nepal. Confusingly, he himself is sometimes depicted issuing from Vishnu's navel or from a golden egg. It is said that he disgraced himself by cheating in an argument with Vishnu and that his deception was made known by a sacred cow.

From time to time, the gods have chosen to appear in human form, as avatars, giving rise to legends in which gods, goddesses, kings, queens, saints, and even animals and trees, are all entwined. The king himself, who holds no position in the hierarchy of the official religion, Hinduism, is nevertheless thought by many to be an incarnation or descendant of the great god Vishnu, although this belief is now officially discouraged. Vishnu's role of preserver of life is, however, a suitable one for a king, and through the ages he has taken on many different forms in his efforts to save the world. He may be worshipped in all these manifestations: as Krishna, the perfect young man, as a fish, a tortoise, a boar, a dwarf, a man-lion, or under his alternative name of Narayan. Whatever his name, he is expected, like most Hindu gods, to have normal sexual appetites, and is therefore provided with a wife, usually Lakshmi, goddess of prosperity.

One of the oldest Vishnu figures in the valley can be visited in the pleasure gardens of Balaju, a small dusty village a few miles outside Kathmandu which has more recently been chosen as the site for a new and equally dusty industrial estate. We went to Balaju primarily to look for a silk mill where both plain and exotically patterned silks were woven by hand on wooden looms, but having first accidentally found our way into a large, noisily modern and impressive, cotton mill, and then to the older shabbier silk factory, were persuaded that we should also pay our respects to Vishnu. We found the god lying flat on his back under a canopy in a little ornate pond, his belly covered with coins thrown in by his faithful followers. The intricately carved figures adorning the roof struts of his temple were unusually modestly attired in loincloths. Nearby, a number of people were bathing in the water from a row of carved spouts protruding from the retaining wall of the largest of a series of more or less stagnant fish tanks; families were picnicking on the grass below a wooded slope which hid unattended cages of antelopes, peacocks, and pheasants. No one else seemed to be paying any attention to Vishnu, whose antiquity is in some doubt: according to various guide books, the figure is either 600 years old, or a copy of another figure of that age which was discovered where it had been buried, possibly for centuries, by a farmer digging his field. Blood is said to have spurted from the ground.

Shiva is even more complicated than Vishnu, "a god of a thousand aspects and names", both destroyer and regenerator. As destroyer, Shiva is worshipped mainly as Bhairab, in one of over sixty different forms. Bhairab is usually fairly easily recognizable; he has many arms, a dreadful fierce expression with fangs and open bulging menacing eyes, is often adorned with skulls and skeletons, and is usually black or dark blue, although we also saw a white Bhairab. If he is neglected he may become angry, with terrible consequences, so he has his own worshippers and his own festivals, and must be appeased and placated regularly. There are probably millions of different images of Bhairab in the country, and each has its own characteristics and even its own wife. For instance, Bhairab of Bhadgaon has as his wife the Goddess Bhadra Kali, one of many forms of the black goddess; the two are fêted together in the Bhadgaon New Year celebrations.

Our first sight of Bhairab was in the Hanuman Dhoka Square, outside the ancient palace where the king was to be crowned. This vast Kal Bhairab – Black Bhairab – is restrained for all but a day of each year behind strong bars. His face is frightening enough to justify the terror that the threat "Bhairab will get you" inspires in Nepalese children. It is said that anyone who tells a lie in front of him will die vomiting blood, and he used to be used as a lie detector for government officials and accused criminals. Another Bhairab sits inside the Hanuman Dhoka itself, and not far away Akash (blue) Bhairab presides over the Indrachok area: he is not quite so huge and awful, but must always look up from his position over the street as anyone upon whom his eyes fall will be instantly destroyed.

Shiva has a good and peaceful side to balance his Bhairab manifestations, and is often portrayed sitting lovingly with his wife, Uma or Parbati, or as the god of music, dance, or wisdom; he adopts many names, among them Pashupati, Mahesvara, Mahadeva and Mahadeo – or Great God.

As the regenerator, sex plays a pretty important part in Shiva's life, and he may take the form of a lingam, usually accompanied by a yoni. The lingam is the phallic symbol, the male organ, unself-consciously displayed as a central part of religious belief and art. It may be a piece of rock or stone which has taken on the phallic shape naturally, or it may be carved from wood or stone, an upright cylinder usually decorated with carvings which often include sacred snakes, or show Shiva's face on all four sides. As the male organ is not much use on its own, the lingam is placed on or near a yoni, a disc-shaped base which represents the femal sexual organ, the energy which turns the passive male organ. Perfection can be achieved in religious terms by perfect union between the two. It is difficult to imagine the Church of England advocating orgasm as the means of entering heaven, or decorating its buildings with explicit symbols of sexual union. Although it may need an exercise of imagination to see that lingams on their yoni bases represent both sexual and philosophical perfection, the sculptures which adorn many temples, particularly on the roof struts holding the pagoda tiers, depict most explicit, unself-conscious, sometimes even, I imagine, physically impossible, sexual exploits, with a zest which is never present in Christian church sculpture. Obscenity and vulgarity are in the eye of the beholder, and there is a profitable tourist trade in reproductions of these figures. A picturesque explanation for these carvings is that they will keep away the goddess of lightning – an unusually puritanical virgin who will not dare approach such sensuality.

Of the other gods which we could identify easily, the most striking were perhaps Hanuman, the monkey god, and Ganesh, the elephant god. Hanuman, son of the wind god, is incredibly ugly: he stands guard outside the Hanuman Dhoka, coloured bright red from head to foot, sheltered from rain and sun by a large umbrella. Ganesh we found more attractive: he is the son of Shiva – who, in spite of his highly active sex life, seems to have fathered few children. With his elephant's trunk, small body, and four arms, Ganesh brings good fortune and success; he is cheerful and fun-loving, wily and cunning, and probably more prayed to than any other god, with many women fasting in his honour every Tuesday. Even Brahma and the sun god Surya have, it is said, prayed to Ganesh.

The most important Hindu temple in the valley is Pashupatinath, dedicated to Shiva as Pashupati, on the banks of the sacred Bagmati river three miles north-east of Kathmandu. To die at Pashupatinath is particularly fortunate, and anyone who manages it can comfort himself in his last hours with the thought of all the advantage he is gaining for his next life. The next best thing to actually dying there is to be cremated at the temple and have one's ashes consigned to the sacred waters, so that eventually the ashes will join the Ganges, holiest of all Hindu rivers.

It was to Pashupatinath that the body of the last king, Mahendra, like the bodies of many kings before him, was brought and ceremonially burnt. In earlier times, he would have had many wives, all of whom would have consigned themselves, alive, to the flames of his funeral pyre in the now abolished practice of *sati.* I find it quite extraordinary to think that either marital devotion or religious piety could ever be so strong that a woman would go through with this particularly painful form of suicide, but history records that on occasion as many as ten or a dozen women died in the flames of one man.

On the day when I visited Pashupatinath with the children, walking from Kathmandu along a dusty street lined with crumbling houses, grey-green trees, and parched grass verges, no fewer than five bodies were being burnt. This was surprising, as people who had lived in Kathmandu for many years and often visited the temple told me that they had rarely seen more than one body at a time, and often none at all. The pyres had already been lit on funeral ghats, little stone platforms built out over the river in front of the temple. As non-Hindus, we were not allowed into the temple precincts, but crossed a stone bridge to the far bank of the river opposite the ghats and the overhanging eaves of the outer temple buildings. Smoke drifted towards us over the muddy undistinguished looking water and hung in the air against the colour bleaching sun; the smell of burning flesh was strange and sharp and after a while nauseating.

Bodies brought to be burnt must always be carried through the water and not over the bridge, and only Hindus may be burnt on the ghats. One pyre had been built on the grass on our side of the river – perhaps because the deceased was a Buddhist, or perhaps because all the ghats were already occupied. A little knot of mourners squatted round the fire, which had only just been lit; we could see the corpse clearly as the smoke rose and the first few flames licked up: an emaciated elderly man, his skinny legs bent at the knee and his arms folded so that, if it had not been for his bed of fire, he could have been a picnicker lying on his back, gazing unseeingly up at the vultures wheeling hopefully overhead. A man in a long white shirt was squatting close to the fire while another carefully shaved his head – the outward symbol of mourning; the women of the group were cooking a chicken over a second fire, as a joint sacrifice and feast.

To my surprise, the children did not find the sight of burning bodies distressing: bodies have, after all, to be disposed of, and this, they agreed, was a practical way of doing it, far healthier than keeping the dead lying around and then burying them. Cremation is cremation, however the ceremony surrounding it is carried out, and the Nepalese approach is no more gruesome than the secrecy surrounding our own crematoria.

Death is hushed up in our society, and I realized that we had rarely, if ever, talked about it with the children: sitting on the grass under the drifting smoke of funeral pyres, we talked about beliefs, about life and death, about differences and similarities. Even Megan, at five, was curious and interested to try to understand the beliefs of other people, and I was glad to find that all three accepted without difficulty that there are many different ways of explaining what cannot be understood – which is, after all, what religion is about – and that religious belief, social necessity, and custom go together. Where life is often short and hard, belief that each life is part of a chain, that reincarnation is possible, and that grace can be gained in one life and carried over into another, is at least comforting – and no less credible than the Christian idea of life after death in a purely spiritual sense.

So we talked for a while, until Megan said, "It's very sensible to burn bodies, but I don't like the smell," and we left the open-air funerals, walking up steep stone steps between trees and monkeys. Stone animals guarded the steps at intervals, and cripples lined the bottom few, begging and wheedling. That it is more blessed to give than to receive is a belief more strongly held and more often acted upon in Hindu and Buddhist life than in the so-called Christian world. By giving alms to beggars, the giver can tot up extra points towards his next reincarnation; but as we passed these beggars, some hideously deformed by leprosy, still widespread in Nepal, or with mis-shapen or missing limbs, I felt ashamed either to give or not to give. Except at a few special places like this one, we saw few beggars in Nepal, although an unfortunate side-effect of the increased prosperity brought by tourists is an increase in begging with its accompanying lowering of pride.

As we climbed, we could see the temple's pagoda roof gleaming golden through the trees, with a cluster of other pagoda-roofed buildings beside it round the temple courtyard. It is claimed that the Nepalese invented the pagoda style, more or less accidentally; first they thought it would be sensible to have a roof over the place where they sacrificed to prevent the rain putting the fire out, but the roof needed a hole in it to allow the smoke to escape; then the rain poured through the hole and put the fire out, so another roof was added above the first. The result was pleasingly elegant, and occasionally more roofs were added, giving artists and craftsmen any number of roof struts to embellish.

One of the most impressive pagoda temples in the valley is the Nyatpolo temple, built for the Malla king Bhupatendra of Bhadgaon in 1708, with five pagoda roofs (Nyatpolo meaning five-roofed) above five wide tiers of steps and terraces guarded by pairs of stone figures in ascending order of spiritual power. The bottom step is guarded by two men, Jaya Malla and Phatta Malla, wrestlers with ten times the strength of other men. Above them are two elephants, ten times more powerful than they are; then two lions, a pair of griffins, and finally the goddesses Baghini and Singhine, tigress and lioness deified. As each pair is ten times stronger than the pair below, the goddesses at the top are a hundred thousand times more powerful than any mere mortal and the god lurking behind the closed temple doors enjoys a million times greater strength than a man.

The strangest of all the Nepalese deities is the Kumari, the Living Goddess, revered and fêted like the other gods but with one difference: the Kumari is alive, a child, a girl chosen to be the temporary body of the goddess Taleju. Patan and Kathmandu each have a Kumari virgin goddess, and the tradition is, says a guide book, "a most unique one in Asia and only to be seen in Nepal," which is probably just as well. Megan, who loves to dress up, was at first envious of the little Kumari virgin goddess in her temple palace with her rich formal clothes and stylized makeup and jewellery: but when she realized that the child could not go out to play and must sit for hours praying and meditating, she decided her life did not sound so tempting after all.

The Kumari is chosen from a small number of eligible Newari children of the goldsmith caste in a series of tests and initiation rites which are supposed to prove her divinity. There are those, cynics and critics, who say that the calmness of the child through experiences which would send most normal children out of their wits merely proves that she is particularly lacking in intelligence and sensitivity. Among other things, she must stay alone for a night in a room filled with animals' heads, monsters and demons. Once chosen, she must be able to sit still for hours on end and should never fidget or show signs of emotion as other children do.

The Kumari remains a goddess until she bleeds, whether through menstruation or from a cut: when blood flows in any way from her body, her divinity also leaves her, and she returns to her family, ill-fitted for any normal life. The family will have benefited financially and socially, but the ex-Kumari will find it hard to marry, as she is considered an unlucky match, and it is said that several ex-Kumaris now lead a life of misery and prostitution. Somehow, the Patan Kumari has remained at her post for many years, long past the time when she could be expected to have menstruated, either because she has not developed normally or through deception.

While she is a goddess, the unfortunate girl is thought to have prophetic powers: even royalty consults her, and each year she grants the king the divine right to rule for another year with a special blessing. It is said that the death of the King Tribhuvan was preceded by an omen from the Kumari: when, during the annual festival of Indra Jatra, he went to receive his blessing and the holy mark of the tika from her, she absentmindedly or instinctively placed the tika on the forehead of his son, Mahendra – and well before Indra Jatra came round again, Tribhuvan was dead and Mahendra king.

The Kumari tradition is relatively new, dating only from the middle of the eighteenth century. During the reign of Jaya Prakash Malla, the last of the Malla kings of Kathmandu, the mother goddess Taleju apparently took on human form, entering the body of a Newari girl. The king banished the girl, thinking it was a trick; but the goddess, determined not to be thwarted, then entered the body of the queen, with such frenzy that the king fetched the girl back to release his wife.

A palace was built for the young goddess, and a special ceremony created for her during the week-long celebrations of the Indra Jatra festival. The king often visited the goddess in the palace which he had given her conveniently near his own, and after a while was attracted to her as a woman rather than as a goddess. This, it is said, was the beginning of the end of the house of Malla, for the goddess took offence and vanished, warning him that he and his dynasty would not last much longer. She ordered that a girl from her people, the Newari, should be selected as the recipient of her spirit, and worshipped as Kumari. Not long after the new goddess had been chosen, the first of the Shah kings of Nepal invaded Kathmandu, on the day of the Kumari's Indra Jatra procession. King Jaya Prakash Malla fled to

Patan, and as Prithvi Narayan Shah was civil enough to allow Kumari's festival to continue, she is said to have indicated divine acceptance of the Shah line by placing the tika on his forehead.

Although Hinduism is the official faith of Nepal, there are many Buddhists in the country. Buddha himself was a Hindu of the ruling class. His name was Gautama Siddhartha, and he was born miraculously from between his mother's ribs, or so it is said, in Lumbini in southern Nepal, more than five centuries before the equally miraculous birth of Jesus Christ. He led a prince's rich and protected life until as a young married man he wandered one evening from his palace and saw the poverty and injustice of the world. Overwhelmed by his sudden knowledge of suffering, he felt compelled to forsake his family and wealth, and set out as a beggar in search of enlightenment on a prolonged pilgrim's progress during which he withstood the tempter Mara, as Christ withstood the temptations of Satan in the wilderness.

At last he understood that he must return to the world, not as a king but as a teacher, and that he could not help others by withdrawing and meditating alone. This was his supreme sacrifice, through which he achieved Nirvana, the state of perfect bliss, unity with God. Until his death at the age of eighty he devoted himself to spreading his message of peace, tolerance, and gentleness, rejecting the elements of Hindu faith which he felt to be negative, such as the division of all people into castes and the practice of human and animal sacrifice. To take life or to make a child cry were, he taught, among the greatest sins.

Buddha did not claim divinity, nor is he worshipped as a god, but through him God is worshipped and the way to God was shown. In the same way, Muslims see Mohammed as a prophet of the indefinable deity, and Christian Catholics use their saints as intermediaries of God. Gautama Buddha was only one of many incarnations of Buddha, or one of several men who have achieved Buddhahood and who therefore pass after death into Nirvana, the ultimate goal of both Buddhists and Hindus.

Of course, most people never achieve this perfection, and so are condemned to return to the world time after time, the idea of reincarnation being central to both Hindu and Buddhist belief. The aim is to reach such saintliness in successive lives that any further incarnations become unnecessary as the perfect soul becomes one with the universal spirit. Imperfect souls must struggle on in body after body, and in each life the individual must behave in such a way that he or she gains good points, *sonam* or grace, for the next. Ancestor worship plays an important part; the souls of the deceased must be given assistance for their future lives, and may be enlisted to support the living. The idea is not far removed from the belief that souls in torment because of some dreadful deed must wander the world as ghosts until somehow their spirit is released, but expressed more tidily, with a greater sense of continuity and an insistence on the responsibility of the individual to make an ever greater effort.

The belief in reincarnation has a positive aspect, explaining the traditional honesty, generosity, and hospitality of the Nepalese, and their frequent elaborate festivals, *jatra*, to please and appease the gods who will decide whether they should be promoted or demoted next time round. It has also, however, given rise to many superstitions and explains the various taboos of Hindu society, such as the "pollution period" after a bereavement or after giving birth and during menstruation, which no doubt grew from some half-understood fear of infection and the belief that to mix with people defiled by any such pollution would detract from the spiritual grace gained by virtuous behaviour.

Buddhism was probably introduced to Nepal during Gautama's lifetime, possibly even by the Buddha himself, and spread across Asia for several hundred years, reaching its height under the Indian emperor Ashoka two hundred and fifty years before the birth of Christ. By the time Buddhism lost its appeal in India it was firmly established in Nepal, Tibet, and China. In Tibet, where ancient animistic beliefs were absorbed, Buddhism remained not only the religion but also the basis of the country's legal and social system until the Chinese imposed communist rule. In Nepal, the Hindu faith, complete with its caste system into which the Buddhists were drawn, was re-established in the middle ages by the Malla kings. Ever since, Hinduism as the official faith has co-existed peacefully with Buddhism.

Few people insist on the literal truth of the thousands of stories loosely based on religion in which historical fact and mythological fantasy involve gods and goddesses, king and queens, holy men and peasants, even animals and plants, fire and water, in adventures which make the Arabian Nights or the Quest for the Holy Grail seem drab and credible. There is a perfectly logical explanation behind many of the myths, but the Nepalese prefer the exuberant poetry and colour of their ancient legends. The creation of the Kathmandu valley and the mountains surrounding it can, for instance, be traced geologically, but the Nepalese version is far more appealing.

Once upon a time, according to both geology and mythology, the Kathmandu valley was a lake, the home of serpents and of Karkotak, king of the serpents. Aeons before the birth of the Gautama Buddha in the south of Nepal – himself, depending on the choice of source, the sixth, fifty-fifth, or even 101st of the Buddhas sent to represent Shoyambhu, the ultimate and indefinable divinity, on earth – this lake was a holy place, a place of miracles and prophecies.

The lake, serene and beautiful, reflecting the Himalayan peaks, homes of the gods, in its deep waters, had one flaw: the lotus would not flower there; until, that is, Shoyambhu, the Self-Existent One, the universal spirit, absolute reality (or God) was revealed in the form of a lotus, which, taking root in an underwater hill, flowered a miraculous flower. This flower gave out a sacred light and the lake became a place of pilgrimage for divine and semi-divine beings.

After many ages had passed, and still long before the birth of Buddha as Gautama, a Bhodisattva or mini-Buddha crossed the mountains from China, drew his sword, and with one mighty blow slashed through the hills surrounding the lake in fulfilment of an ancient prophecy. The waters flowed out through the gash which is now known as the Chobar Gorge and through which the valley rivers still flow to join the sacred waters of the Ganges.

The valley thus created was fertile, enjoying relatively flat land and a pleasant climate, and became the home of farmers, builders and artists. Some say the Bhoddisattva – the title given to one who aspires to and is near attaining Buddhahood – was Manjusri, Buddha of the five Chinese peaks; others say he was the great Hindu God Vishnu, as Narayan. Many say they are one and the same anyway, and no one really minds.

On the hill on which the lotus took root there now stands the temple of Swayambhu, or Shoyambhu; it is claimed that Swayambhunath was built over 2,000 years ago, within a few centuries of the birth of Buddha, and that it is the oldest Buddhist temple in the world; but even so there are Hindu shrines, to the goddesses of learning and of smallpox, beside it.

We could see Swayambhunath on its hill on the far side of the city from the Waterhouses' windows, and soon after we returned from trekking the children and I crossed Kathmandu for a closer look. The hilltop, said by one guide book to be 125 feet high and by another 250 feet, can be reached either by road, winding past monastery buildings where monkeys, for some reason sacred, leap from roof to roof or tree to tree chattering and grumbling, or by climbing 300 steep stone steps. A pair of god-sized brilliant yellow inscrutable Buddhas watch over the bottom of the steps, which are guarded by stone animals, also in pairs, in ascending order of power – lions, horses, elephants – with live monkeys playing disrespectfully over them.

The central building at the top is the Buddhist stupa, a great gleaming white dome above which the Buddha's so-called benevolent face gazes over Kathmandu, under a golden cupola. Round it is a higgledy-piggledy conglomeration of shrines, sculptures, temples, shops, stalls, people, and animals, a typically Nepalese mixture of religion and commerce. We allowed ourselves to be lured into the tourist trap of the souvenir trade. "For you, it is a very good price today – we have not many customers now so you can have things at Nepalese prices – for Americans it is more expensive, and for Germans, but this is not a good time of year for tourists." Dogs and goats, as well as monkeys, wandered freely in and out of shrines. One dog, little more than a mangy skeleton, held together by scabby skin hanging from its bones, lay down in front of us in a shrine – and was dead.

Weird unearthly music from the main temple drew us up broad steps to look through the open door into the gloom. Although the inner sanctum of a Hindu temple may not be entered by non-believers, for fear of defilement, the same does not apply to Buddhist places of worship, where all are made welcome. We were beckoned in by a shaven-headed monk dressed in the traditional saffron robes of the Buddhist priesthood. Other monks were sitting in two rows, the back row raised above the front on a dais; twin strings of fairy lights flashed incongruously on and off behind them, giving the impression of a gaudy three-dimensional semi-animated tableau. Facing the door was an elaborate pyramid of wool, straw, and paper flowers constructed round a Buddha figure, and fastened to the pyramid, like macabre Christmas decorations, were paper cut-outs of more Buddhas and of skulls. Little dishes of beans, rice and spices were spread out as offerings at its feet.

The monks were chanting low and deep in their throats. Every few minutes, the chanting gave way to beating on vast belly throbbing drums and strange penetrating wailing from a huge collapsible horn. The monks raised the drums on long handles, beating them in unison with curved bows while another monk walked between them waving a brass bowl of incense. The sound was quite unearthly, but intoxicating, and I found the effect on me almost alarming; it seemed to rise from the ground into my bones and my brain, surrounding and enveloping me, and producing an unfamiliar feeling of deep calm coupled with intense excitement. If religious experience can be separated from religious belief or understanding, then this was such an experience.

We made our way back down the steep straight steps between the stone animals, turning every now and then to look back at Buddha's impersonal compelling benevolent eyes high above us under gaily coloured flags. At the bottom of the slope, near the giant Buddhas, little family groups were squatting on the grass or wandering under the trees as they supervised their grazing buffalo and goats. Three elephants were being guarded at a little distance from the other animals, and were eating peacefully, munching their way at an alarming rate through huge bundles of foliage which a man in a tree above them was cutting and throwing down. There are usually no elephants in the valley, but thirty had been brought up to Kathmandu from the tropical Terai for the coronation. As nearly half of them had succumbed to some form of foot and mouth disease, it did not seem as if the altitude (4,000 feet higher than what they were used to) agreed with them – which judging from the denuded state of the trees they were being fed from was probably just as well.

Swayambhu is a couple of miles outside Kathmandu, and we walked back through narrow streets where many of the inhabitants were Tibetan. One street, empty and dusty in front of the doors and

Restoration work inside the Hanuman Dhoka in Kathmandu. The scaffolding is made of bamboo

Families work together and bring their children to the tile and brick fields in the Kathmandu valley

A potter at Thimi

Traditional pottery on sale in the Kathmandu bazaar

Bodi Raj Sakya, sculptor, working in 'lost wax' tradition in his home in Patan

In the silk mill at Balaju industrial estate outside Kathmandu

Statue outside a temple

Below: Temple buildings and funeral ghats at Pashupatinath. On the left the body of a Hindu is being burnt on a ghat

Buddha's four-sided benevolent face above the stupa at Bodnath, decorated with flags for the Tibetan New Year

Below: Tibetan man in front of the shrine in the lower wall of Bodnath's stupa

Temple restoration undertaken by men as well as women from the Newari people

At the temple of Bajra Jogini above the Newari village of Sankhu on the edge of the Kathmandu valley

Newari craftsman working in the woodworkers' area of Patan

Ancient Newari craftsmanship. Their elaborate carvings can still be seen above doors and windows and on temples in the valley

A photo taken by the Rana court photographer in about 1938, when the Rana family was still in control of Nepal

Family gathering, 1946. It was still the custom for the wealthy to have several wives and mistresses

windows of tall terraced houses, echoed with a dull clack-clack of wood rhythmically hitting wood; Tibetan carpets were being made in the front rooms on foot- and hand-powered semi-automated looms. Turning the corner, we had to step carefully round some women who had stretched their weaving from one end to the other of the street, and were busily moving along a narrow length of striped cloth. In the open space between houses at a crossroads more women were weaving, spinning, and winding wool.

Soon we were walking past the back yards of a row of Nepalese laundries, or *dhobi*. Washing was being scrubbed and banged outside, behind the houses, with pails of water fetched from a communal pump. Spotlessly clean laundry was hung from a line, draped over bushes, and even spread on the ground to dry. Not far from the laundries we passed a small one-man pottery in a dilapidated single-storey mat shack. Wearing only a long white shirt and squatting over his wheel, a large rubber tyre set in the ground and driven by occasional flicks from a wooden paddle, the potter was throwing small dishes for curd very fast from a hump of clay; a few deft movements, a squeeze, and another dish joined the rows set out in the sun to dry.

Much of the area between Swayambhu and the bridge over the Vishnumati River back into Kathmandu was the sort of scruffy no-man's land, unplanned semi-suburbia semi-slum, which develops on the edge of cities everywhere. City life began again on the bridge, where we sat for a while eating peanuts bought from an old man. Below us, the water was dirty and muddy, but nevertheless a group of women were washing their clothes and their hair, sharing a dried mud island left in the middle of the river with some buffalo; the women did not seem worried that the buffalo were walking over the washing they had just spread out to dry. Under the bridge, a buffalo had died, and its empty carcass was being scavenged by a mangy yellow dog whose tail could just be seen wagging inside the rib cage.

Although Swayambhu, gleaming on its hill dominating the city, is impressive, our favourite temple was another great Buddhist shrine, the stupa of Bodnath a few miles outside Kathmandu. Some guide books claim as great or even greater antiquity for the stupa as for Swayambhu, but the most reliable of the modern books I have found (Rishikesh Shaha's *An Introduction to Nepal*) points out that there is no proof of its existence before the seventeenth century. The claim that it is the largest Buddhist shrine in the world is probably more accurate.

Inevitably, the stupa's origins are told in a mixture of fact and myth, kings and gods. Once upon a time, there was a prince of Nepal who had in a previous life been a Tibetan lama. The king, his father, had built a splendid new aqueduct, but no water would run from its spouts. The only way water could be induced to flow was apparently through a supreme sacrifice: the king therefore ordered his son to go to the waterless tap and behead the man he would find there wrapped in a sheet – thus calling upon the prince to commit unwitting patricide and sacrificing himself to satisfy the gods.

The prince, as a good son must, obeyed his father's order; when he discovered whom he had beheaded, he was so horrified that he retired from public life to meditate. The goddess of the temple to which he withdrew told him that his crime would be expiated if he built a great temple to Buddha, and that a white crane would settle on the site for this offering. The crane settled at Bodnath, and as the prince decided that his temple should be the largest Buddhist shrine in the world the colossal stupa rose gradually from the flat ground, and is now the greatest Tibetan and Buddhist gathering place in Nepal – and probably, since the closure of the Potala in Lhasa, in the world.

For once, there is no mixture of creeds and shrines at Bodnath, the stupa rising from the ground uncluttered and totally improbable. In the walls dozens of prayer wheels are set in niches, and beside wide stone steps leading to the curve of the dome is a rich-looking shrine behind bars. There always seem to be several plump rats scurrying round behind the bars among the offerings of food put out for the Buddha – or for them; it is difficult to tell. They certainly know when they are on to a good thing, as no one will harm them, killing even such lowly creatures being in Buddhist belief a sin.

Two circular walks above the wall of prayer wheels lead round the base of the stupa dome, which, perfect and unclimbable, would make St Paul's look insignificant. Above the dome, Buddha's strange eyes gaze in all four directions from a square stone tower, with a question mark of a nose which gives him a surprised rather than a benevolent expression. The four-sided face symbolizes "universal compassion for all sentient beings". As it was near the Buddhist New Year, bright strings of flags had somehow been attached to the very top of the stupa, where they fluttered cheerfully across Buddha's faces, looking less incongruous than the telephone wires stretched irreverently under his noses.

Four curved terraces of tall thin houses, separated by four narrow approach streets, surround the stupa and are the homes of Tibetan traders, who sell a variety of old and not so old Tibetan and Nepalese curios: jewels, ornaments, strange musical instruments, heavy dusty clothes. It is difficult to resist the persuasive sales talk of dark tangle-haired Tibetan women in long thick skirts and bright woollen aprons, or men with their hair in untidy pigtails, the roughness of their clothes, usually long heavy robes, often belied by expensive modern wrist-watches. Aggressive little Tibetan mountain dogs yap at strangers and are best avoided.

Although there are so many hundreds and even thousands of religious buildings in Nepal, it seems there is always room for more, and a large new monastery was being built not far from Bodnath's stupa. The building was already structurally completed, a plain rectangular barrack-like block with bleak cement facing about to be embellished with traditional bright Buddhist designs. Inside, workmen were busy painting the walls with god-sized symbols and figures. A colossal new Buddha already sat in his most favoured position, one hand touching the ground, the other on his lap, his fingers elegantly splayed and stretched; on either side of him sat another vast Buddha figure in a different pose.

The Tibetan Buddhist New Year, held on the day of the full moon in February, is of course celebrated with due ceremony at Bodnath. From dusk, the faithful walk in a clockwise direction – to walk anti-clockwise is insulting – round the stupa, sometimes prostrating themselves in the street, spinning the prayer wheels as they pass so that thousands of invisible prayers are sent fluttering up to heaven. The Chinai Lama, the spiritual head of the Buddhist faith in Nepal (and, I have been told, an enthusiastic bargainer and businessman) officiates, with complicated prayers, ritual bellringing, and the giving of strips of red cloth in blessing. When the full moon is high in the sky Buddhists carrying lighted wicks and lamps process round the stupa chanting prayers of thanksgiving.

10

Shahs and Ranas

Nepal's history is as complicated as its religion, the lack of accurate documentation and the frequent interference of the gods making it difficult to sort out fact from fiction. Quite how the commonly held but officially denied belief that the Shah is a reincarnation of Vishnu arose I have no idea. As the date of the coronation drew nearer, I tried to put the impending historic event into some sort of perspective, not helped by the frequent confusion about dates: the Nepalese have their own calendar, in which they were already well past the year 2,000, and hop from this to the Gregorian calendar in their accounts of the past, often losing or gaining a year or two on the way, so that several quite different dates are often given for the same event.

Very little is known about the early history of Nepal, which until its unification in the eighteenth century consisted of many separate small kingdoms. The name Nepal was first recorded in the ninth century, and referred only to the area of the Kathmandu valley. Even the valley history until the Middle Ages is a matter of guesswork. The first people known to have inhabited it are the Kirantis, the probable ancestors of the Newaris. The Kirantis were the rulers of the valley at the time of the birth of Gautama Buddha in the sixth century B.C., and under them the Buddhist faith was established in Nepal. No one knows where they came from or who was there before them.

Even less is known about their successors, the Licchavis, who are thought to have come from India some time in the first few centuries A.D.; the only contemporary written mention of them is on a fifth-century pillar at Changunarayan. In the seventh century, the Thakuris, Indian Hindus, became the valley rulers. The daughter of the first Thakuri ruler, the emperor Amshuvarman, is popularly supposed to have married the legendary Tibetan King Tsong Tsen

Gampa, founder of Lhasa, and it is thought that Nepal came under Tibetan dominance for a while.

From the early thirteenth century until the late eighteenth century, the rulers of the valley and at times of a considerably wider area were the Hindu Mallas, who again came north from India. The seventh Malla king, Jayastithi, institutionalized the Hindu caste system, dividing even the Buddhists, who originally rejected such distinctions, into no fewer than eighty-four castes. Under the eighth Malla, Yaksha, the kingdom of Nepal was extended, but on his death – which was in 1488 or 1459, depending on the source of information – it was divided between his sons. The valley remained split into separate Malla kingdoms, and at times in the next two centuries there were literally dozens of individual principalities outside the valley. Culturally, the Mallas were a good thing. Under their patronage the arts and crafts of the Newari valley people flourished, and the valley towns they created are still a delight.

While Mallas were enlarging and then subdividing their kingdom, not far from the valley another tribe from India, warlike Rajput Kshatriyas, were growing in strength. From 1559, these high-caste people, driven north from India in the fourteenth century by the Muslims, made their headquarters in Gorkha, under their Shah ruler. The ninth Gorka Shah, Prithvi Narayan, inherited the throne in 1742 at the age of twelve and for the next twenty-five years tried to achieve his father's unfulfilled ambition of becoming king of Kathmandu. If the separate valley Malla kings had combined their forces, he probably would not have beaten them; but as they didn't one by one they were defeated. One of the Malla kings asked the British for help from India, but the British soldiers were no match for Nepal's malarial mosquito and the Gurkha soldiers. By 1769, Prithvi Narayan was Shah king of Kathmandu and the other valley cities, and within a few years his kingdom included the whole of modern Nepal.

Prithvi Narayan Shah's rule is generally seen now as a good thing, in spite of the notorious siege of Kirtipur towards the end of his campaign to conquer the valley. Kirtipur, a little city on a hill, was surrounded but refused to surrender until Prithvi Narayan promised clemency. As soon as the Kirtipurians opened the city gates, he ordered his soldiers to cut the nose off of every male inhabitant, except, with a bizarre sense of mercy, those who played wind instruments. Punishment by mutilation was common, but even so this brutality was unusually excessive.

After the death of Prithvi Narayan, Shah rule gradually deteriorated. Shah No. 2, Pratap Singh Shah, imprisoned his brother; Shah No. 3, Ran Bahadur, came to the throne when he was three years old, under an ambitious uncle who ruled until the king was old enough to imprison him. Ran Bahadur Shah is said to have been "debauched, useless, a criminal lunatic", and after eleven years abdicated on behalf of his son, Shah No. 4, another infant king, Girvana Yuddha. If the dates most commonly given are accurate, Ran Bahadur was only fourteen when he handed over to Girvana, who died in 1816. During most of Girvana's reign, the prime minister, Bhim Sen Thapa, apparently both an enlightened reformer and a homicidal maniac, did most of the ruling; he is commemorated in Kathmandu by the Bhim Tower, a singularly useless monument like a landlocked white lighthouse. Bhim Sen Thapa was still prime minister during the early years of Shah No. 5, Rajendra – who is described as "weak, vacillating", not to mention "jealous and demented".

Bhim Sen Thapa maintained his position as prime minister against strong and jealous opposition from a rival family, the Pandes, until 1837, when an ambitious Pande and the equally ambitious junior queen, Lakshmi Devi, conspired to have him imprisoned. The king released but then re-imprisoned him, and Bhim eventually cut his throat with his kukhri in prison. In the next nine years, there were at least nine changes in government.

It was the custom for kings (and others) to have more than one wife, not to mention mistresses. Queens, concubines, advisers, regents, and social climbers, grouped in rival factions; intrigue and murder to gain power were common; political integrity and stability virtually unknown. Rajendra had two wives; by his senior queen he had two sons, Surendra and Upendra. In 1843, the Shah handed over his powers to his junior queen, Lakshmi Devi. The senior queen was already dead, but the following year he granted her son Surendra certain royal prerogatives, and then further confused the issue by sometimes supporting the queen, sometimes the prince. The queen's chief concern was the advancement of her low-caste lover, Gagan Singh, whom she elevated to the position of commander of seven regiments and the army's arsenals.

Queen Lakshmi Devi soon felt that the prime minister, Mathbar Singh Thapa (appointed by Rajendra, still nominally Shah), was altogether too powerful. She therefore arranged for him to be shot by his nephew and protégé at court, a young man called Jang Bahadur. Later, Jang Bahadur Rana (as he subsequently became known) is said to have commented on his victim's portrait: "That is my poor uncle, Mathbar Singh, whom I shot; it is very like him." The assassination took place in May 1845, and as a reward the queen made Jang Bahadur commander of a quarter of the Nepalese army.

Eighteen months later, the king decided to exercise his royal and conjugal rights by removing his wife's lover from the scene. At 10 p.m. on 14th September 1846 Gagan Singh was consequently shot dead at his prayers. The queen reacted passionately, summoning the court instantly to the Kot, the meeting place in national or royal emergency.

Jang Bahadur arrived first, backed up by his troops. No one has established exactly what happened during the night of the "Kot massacre", but by morning Jang Bahadur was prime minister and commander in chief of the army, the street outside the Kot was running with blood, and several hundred people inside the Kot were dead. This, although no one realized it at the time, marked the end of active Shah rule for a century, and the start of the Rana regime; almost anything, as Jang Bahadur was well aware, would be better than the chaos under Shah No. 5.

Queen Lakshmi Devi had a son, Ranendra, whom she wished to put on the thrown. She therefore ordered her new prime minister to assassinate the heir to the throne and his brother, Surendra and Upendra. Jang Bahadur refused, made the crown prince Surendra Shah, and with his young highness's approval both Rajendra and Lakshmi Devi were exiled. One of the most extraordinary facets of the Rana regime was that none of the Rana rulers ever acted specifically against the king, and that Jang Bahadur established the Rana dictatorship legally and with the king's agreement, although it effectively removed all power from the Shahs.

The name of Rana, which Jang Bahadur took for himself and his family, put him on a social level with the Shah family. The Rajput Ranas of Rajasthan were a famous Indian royal house, and the Nepalese Ranas made themselves the equals of royalty as Chetris on the caste ladder, availing themselves freely of the resulting right to marry Shah princes and princesses.

In 1850, after four years as prime minister, during which he had become increasingly powerful, Jang Bahadur Rana visited England, on the first Nepalese state visit to any western country. He travelled under the grand title of His Excellency the Nepalese Ambassador Jang Bahadur Rana, with a suitably magnificent retinue which included two of his younger brothers and twenty-five servants. Queen Victoria received him and granted him the Order of the Bath, as a result of which it was widely assumed in Nepal that he was her lover – why else would she have received him in the bathroom? Jang Bahadur visited mines, farms, hospitals, army and navy establishments, and the opera (which impressed him least). While he was in London, an attempt was made on Queen Victoria's life; he was astonished that the culprit was neither executed nor mutilated, which would have been considered just punishment in Kathmandu.

Jang Bahadur Rana had six younger brothers, to whom he gave the highest positions in the land. While he was in England (and France, which he visited on his way back) he left one of them, Bam Bahadur Rana, in charge. During his absence, another brother, Badri Narsingh, plotted against him with the Shah's brother. On his return, Jang Bahadur surprised the Nepalese court by putting into practice his respect for the British way of doing things by merely banishing the offending brother.

It was not long before a group of influential dignitaries, no doubt impressed by the unusual stability and mildness of Jang Bahadur's rule and wishing to curry favour, offered him the crown. He refused, being "not at all disposed to fill the place of one whom I myself have put upon the throne", and preferring to "supervise the work of government without the gaudy encumbrance of the crown".

He was, however, quite willing to accept from the Shah the hereditary title of "Maharaja", and to establish the right to pass this title with the position of prime minister from Rana to Rana. In 1856, ten years after the Kot massacre, the Rana succession was granted royal approval in an edict which gave Jang Bahadur and the subsequent Rana prime ministers official power over the royal family and the country.

Jang Bahadur had seen the chaos caused by the succession of rulers too young to rule. He therefore established that Rana power would be handed from eldest male to eldest male, rather than from father to son, hoping that this would ensure greater political stability. If the Ranas who followed him had been of his stature, the Rana regime would have been a good thing. During his thirty years in office it was certainly an improvement. Although illiterate when he came to power he was an able politician, an accomplished soldier, horseman, and athlete, and to some extent a reformer: he abolished some of the worst excesses of previous rulers, made punishment by mutilation illegal, and limited the range of crimes for which the death sentence was automatic.

He was also undoubtedly personally ambitious. Shortly after putting the Rana regime on an official basis, he handed over his position to the next of his six brothers, Bam Bahadur, who died a few months later. Rana No. 3, Krishna Bahadur, followed for a few months; but Jang Bahadur discovered that his influence as Big Brother was less than he had hoped, particularly in dealings with the British, Nepal's neighbour in India, and resumed his position as head of state, remaining in dictatorial power until his death in 1877.

For thirty years, Jang Bahadur Rana ruled over the country and even over the king. Throughout the Rana regime, the king remained a puppet figurehead. Jang Bahadur encouraged the belief that the Shah was a reincarnation of Vishnu, and must therefore be protected from the dangers of political life. The Ranas ensured his safety most effectively and Surendra Bir Bikram Shah was still nominally king when Jang Bahadur died.

Although he officially discouraged sati, three wives committed themselves to Jang Bahadur's funeral pyre on the banks of the Bagmati. After his death, his fifth and eldest surviving brother, Ranodip Singh, succeeded him, according to the law of Rana succession. If the brief rule of brothers 2 and 4 are counted, Ranodip was Rana No. 4. During his rule, Surendra died and his six-year-old son, Prithvi Bir Bikram Shah, inherited the futile luxury of the throne.

The youngest Rana brother, Dhir Shamsher, died without coming to power; but he had seventeen sons. His eldest son, Bir Shamsher, became Rana No. 5 by assassinating Ranodip eight years after Jang Bahadur's death. Rana succession was not working as smoothly as Jang had planned, and his own sons were intensely jealous of the seventeen brothers, their cousins. Maharaj Bir Shamsher Jang Bahadur Rana (each ruler took the founder Rana's full title) removed Jang Bahadur's sons from the roll of succession. Later Ranas made similar alterations in favour of their immediate families.

During his six years in power, Bhir Shamsher JBR (Jang Bahadur Rana) exiled a brother who plotted against him, built several palaces to the greater glory of the Rana name, a clock tower and a suspension bridge, introduced piped water in the valley, opened a school and started a music festival in the Terai. He was followed by Rana No. 7, his brother Dev Shamsher JBR, who had enlightened ideas, founded the first Nepalese newspaper, emancipated female slaves, and planned to introduce secondary education. After only a few months his brothers, fearing a lessening of Rana privilege, forced him to resign in the king's presence, and exiled him to India, where he died thirteen years later in 1913. Rana No. 7, Chandra, another of the seventeen brothers, took over when Dev was banished.

By this time – 1901, fifty years after the start of the Rana regime – there were so many Ranas that it was becoming difficult to ensure that they all had suitably elevated positions in the country. The Ranas, like the Shahs, married many wives, took many mistresses, and so had many children. Chandra decided to sort them out, thus unwittingly hastening the family's eventual downfall, by dividing all Ranas into three classes: A class Ranas, the sons of lawful marriage between equal castes, could be on the roll of succession, were automatically generals at the age of twenty-one, and had all the top jobs. B class Ranas were also legitimate offspring but of marriages between unequal castes, were eligible for slightly less elevated positions, and could aspire no higher than the rank of lieutenant-colonel. The children of concubines were C class Ranas, could rise only to second lieutenant, and although they still had preference over non-Ranas could not expect to become very influential. As early as 1903, two years after Chandra divided his many relatives into these categories, disgruntled C class Ranas started to form jealous groups in defiance of their A class brothers and cousins.

Chandra was in power until 1929, and made a start on long-needed reforms: he abolished sati and slavery; reduced corruption in the civil service; expanded primary education; initiated land reform; built a few roads and introduced electricity in the valley; and made a ropeway over the mountains so that luxuries imported for the wealthy minority (the Ranas) did not have to be carried across the mountains by porters. His reforms were chiefly of benefit to the Ranas, and on his death he managed to leave £40 million while the majority of the people had no income at all, but at least it was a start.

During Chandra's term of office, Shah No. 8, Tribhuvan Bir Bikram Shah, grandfather of the present king, succeeded to the throne. He, like the sixth and seventh Shahs, was kept a virtual prisoner from his accession in 1911. Maharaj Chandra JBR was followed by two more brothers, Bhim Shamsher JBR (1929-32) and Juddha JBR (1932-46). Juddha had sixteen sons and sixteen daughters, among them both A and C class Ranas, and used the country's resources to provide for his enormous family. He also removed C class Ranas from the roll of succession to posts in district administration, which until then had kept most of them happy: when they found their birth no longer automatically entitled them to any sort of privileged employment, they felt there was nothing to lose by plotting against their A class relatives. Another unintentional step had been taken towards the end of Rana supremacy.

Although both the early Shahs and the Ranas practised a deliberate policy of isolationism, helped by the natural barriers of the Himalayas in the north and the malarial swamps and jungles of the Terai in the south, there had been a British resident in Kathmandu before the start of the Rana regime. Each British resident accepted whichever Rana was in power as the country's rightful ruler, as did the British government in India. The approval of Britain safeguarded the regime: but opposition to Rana rule was growing in India. Juddha evoked more opposition than any of his predecessors, and in 1940 the first open criticism was expressed in Nepal by an organization called the Nepal Praja Parishad. Anti-Rana leaflets demanding reform were distributed in Kathmandu disguised as religious pamphlets. In 1941, Juddha sentenced four leaders of the anti-Rana movement to death, four to life imprisonment, and imprisoned a further twenty-six, with the king's agreement – he and King Tribhuvan were outwardly on good terms.

To a limited extent Juddha carried on Chandra's reforms. By the time he abdicated, in 1946, there were a few rice mills, a jute mill and a match factory, a bank, some medical facilities in the valley, and two

Nepali literary magazines. But it was clear that the next Rana would have to make considerable changes if the regime were to survive.

Rana No. 10, Padma Shamsher JBR, a son of Rana No. 5 and first of the third generation to rule, came to office in 1946. In 1947, the year the British left India, a Nepali National Congress Party was formed by exiles in India, and there was a strike at the jute mill at Biratnagar in the Terai, near the Indian border. Both the new Indian government to the south, and the Chinese to the north, had made it clear that they did not approve of Rana rule. Padma JBR realized that some concessions must be made, and drew up a constitution recognizing civil rights without lessening Rana power and privilege.

Even this limited effort was unacceptable to the other Ranas, who forced Padma to resign, putting his cousin Mohan JBR in his place as Rana No. 11. Mohan refused to take any notice of the growing pressure for change from both sides of the Indian border. In Calcutta, exiled C class Ranas were planning an invasion to reinstate the king, supported both by the Indian press and by the Nepali Congress Party. In September 1950 there were riots in Kathmandu; by November there were armed raids across the border from India.

King Tribhuvan was still kept under strict supervision, and was, not surprisingly, refused permission to go to India. However, his request to take his family for a picnic in the valley on 6th November 1950 seemed harmless enough and he was allowed to leave his palace with two royal cars, his three sons (including his heir, Mahendra), and his grandson Birendra. Instead of going for a picnic, he went straight to the Indian Embassy, where he stayed for the next few days.

Mohan JBR made an attempt to maintain his position as ruler over and maker of kings by putting Tribhuvan's three-year-old grandson Gyanendra on the throne. The king, however, had considerable popular support, the ruse failed, and the Shah was flown in an Indian plane to Delhi, where Nehru recognized him as Nepal's rightful ruler.

Tribhuvan returned to Nepal in February 1951. His bloodless coup had ended the Rana regime and reinstated Shah rule. Rana rule is now officially felt to have been the black period of Nepal's history. Mohan remained in office as an unpopular prime minister until the summer, when the king took over direct rule with a council of ministers directly responsible to the throne. He promised general elections by the end of 1952, but the political situation was so unstable that governments came and went in rapid succession until his death in Switzerland, where he was being treated for heart trouble, in 1955. He was succeeded by Mahendra, who again promised elections, which eventually took place in 1959. The congress party won a resounding victory, gaining seventy-three out of 109 seats in the lower house, but the government was short-lived. Within a year of the election, King Mahendra dissolved parliament, throwing the elected prime minister, B.P. Koirala, into prison, and resumed control himself, appointing a council of ministers. This, he claimed, was in the interests of "unity, national integrity, and sovereignty". In 1962 he initiated the partyless panchyat system, under which the king had ultimate control over a government which included a proportion of members of his choice, the rest being representatives elected by various organizations and by district councils, or panchayat.

Mahendra, who inspired great affection among his people, died of a heart attack in January 1972. Birendra was then twenty-five and inherited a kingdom which was still economically and politically backward but which had somehow always managed to remain independent, and a constitution giving him absolute authority and making political parties illegal. His wife is a Rana. Although Rana rule was emphatically ended by the revolution in 1950, by then Ranas and Shahs were so inextricably mixed by marriage that Birendra is descended from both Jang Bahadur and Juddha JBR. There are still Ranas in high positions but this is no longer their automatic right.

Nepal has never been colonized but because of the country's position between India and China outside influences have inevitably been felt, in spite of the sealed border policy of the early Shahs and the Ranas. There was a Chinese embassy in Kathmandu as early as A.D. 646, and the Thakuri king of Nepal Narendra and the Chinese emperor in Peking are recorded as having exchanged gifts of friendship in A.D. 651, a custom which continued off and on into this century. In 1793, Chinese troops attempted to invade Nepal; I have read accounts of this effort which give conflicting results. According to one, most of the Chinese died of typhoid before reaching the Kathmandu valley, four survivors carrying on towards the capital as ambassadors; but they too died, after a long and strenuous march, and were buried within sight of the city. The humps of their graves are not far from the British ambassador's holiday residence at Kakani, only a few hours' walk from Kathmandu. Another version of the invasion story says that the Chinese beat the Gurkhas twenty miles north of Kathmandu and signed a peace treaty, before retreating magnanimously but leaving military stations along the Tibetan border. Afterwards, a Nepalese mission went to Peking every five years, stopping in Lhasa *en route* and taking eighteen months for the round trip.

Tibet and Nepal have had more or less cordial relations, principally for trade, for many centuries, which only ceased when the Chinese sealed the Tibetan border. At various times, one or other country was the dominant partner, but neither seriously interfered with the freedom of the other for long. In the eighteenth century Prithvi Narayan's soldiers looted Tibetan monasteries – the Chinese invasion of Nepal in 1793 was in support of the Tibetans' objections both to this and to the Nepalese demand for a tribute. In 1855 Jang Bahadur's troops entered Tibet; this resulted in a treaty a year later under which the Dalai Lama agreed to pay a tribute of 10,000 rupees and accepted a Nepalese resident in Lhasa. There was already a well-respected Newari community of artists, craftsmen and traders in Lhasa, and many of Lhasa's treasures were created by Newaris. Trade between Nepal and Tibet slumped in 1950, when the Chinese took control in Tibet, and ceased after the Tibetan uprising in 1959. Among the many Tibetans who fled over the mountains to Nepal were the Khambas, whose warlike reputation and anti-Chinese border activities caused annoyance to the Chinese and therefore embarrassment to the Nepalese government.

During the years between the unification of Nepal and British withdrawal from India, Britain rather than India was politically the southern neighbour. In 1767, the British East India Company was asked by the Mallas for help against Prithvi Narayan Shah's invading Gurkha soldiers. Then in 1800 the Shah asked for British military assistance against his prime minister; a year later the Nepalese government signed a treaty allowing the East India Company trading rights and a British resident in Nepal. Between 1814 and 1816 British and Gurkha troops fought along the Nepalese border; in spite of their superior number and weapons, the British found their opponents more of a match than they had expected. They did however eventually defeat the Gurkhas, and could then probably have added Nepal to their empire. Instead, they signed the Treaty of Segauli, which gave the East India Company part of the Terai, and began unofficially to recruit Gurkhas into the British army.

The Terai territory was returned to Nepal in 1857 in gratitude for Nepalese assistance during the Indian border mutiny, and Gurkha recruitment into the British army became official. In the First World War, 20 Gurkha battalions fought with the British; in the Second World War there were 45 Gurkha battalions in the British army. When the British left India, 6 Gurkha regiments stayed with the Indian army and 4 in British service, and it is only since then that Gurkha recruitment has been cut back.

Under Rana rule, British dignitaries were occasionally invited across the sealed borders to take part in the favourite pastime of the Nepalese rulers: big game shooting in the Terai. George V spent ten days as the guest of Chandra JB Rana, who gathered 600 elephants and 10,000 Gurkhas to assist in the sport. The king apparently shot 21 tigers, 10 rhinos, and 2 bears. More recently, when the Duke of Edinburgh was invited to take part in a smaller version of the royal shoot, he developed a diplomatic blister on his trigger finger – he was, after all, president of the world wildlife preservation society.

Many of the Rana and Shah shooting parties were recorded in the photos of the first official court photographer. Towards the end of our time in Kathmandu, we met his grandson, Bala Krishna Sham, a remarkably young-looking man of over seventy who was himself for some time court photographer under the later Ranas but had given up photography to concentrate on painting and writing and his position as president of the Nepalese Academy.

Bala Krishna Shamsher Rana, to give him his full title – he preferred to drop the Rana – welcomed us courteously to his white house on the edge of Kathmandu: his wife brought us strong sweet tea in a living room which was more like a small exotic museum. A huge gilded mirror reflected elaborate panelling and plasterwork, a valuable collection of miniatures, many of which he had made himself, in glass-fronted showcases, and a wall hung with his own paintings.

Photos taken by three generations of court photographers – his grandfather, his father, and Bala Krishna Sham himself – were stored in apparently careless disorder in a little room off the living room. We were shown the huge glass plate camera used by his grandfather: this was brought into Nepal over the mountains in 1870, and at first the glass plate negatives had to be carried back over the mountains to be developed in Calcutta.

A bewildering succession of Shahs and Ranas in stiff formal poses in their even stiffer state dress were pulled from the piles of photographs on a table, on shelves, and on the window sill. Family groups, among them some of Bala Krishna Sham's own family, included wives, concubines, and children in a confusing complexity of relationships. "That is my father, with his wives," Bala Krishna Sham told us of one group. Another showed Juddha Shamsher Jang Bahadur Rana sitting on a rhino which he had shot, surrounded by four Bengal tigers (which he had also shot), and ten assorted wives and concubines.

Some of the photos showed the wealthy interiors of the palaces which the Ranas had built themselves, with rich furnishings and crystal chandeliers imported over the mountains. Others were of the parties in the Terai, with the carefully selected guests of the aristocracy – we identified Lord Curzon, Lord Linlithgow, the Archduke Ferdinand of Austria. Dead rhinos and tigers were lined up in such numbers that it is surprising there was anything left to shoot.

Few of these photos, which record a lifestyle which can never return, have been published outside Nepal. They make a telling contrast to our own photos taken in the villages, where the power struggles of the aristocracy in the valley had little effect on the lives of the people.

11

A Second Trek

It is possible to tire of even the most exotic sightseeing, and after a while my question each morning of "What shall we do today?" began to be met with the answer: "Anything you like – but no temples!" Time was passing pleasantly enough, but there was still almost a whole country to be seen, and the children were as keen as I was to experience more of village and hill life away from the valley. Even Megan, who had at first needed to keep her sense of belonging somewhere safe and easily identifiable by constant harping back to tiny details of school life, had been sorry when our trek ended. When I told David that I intended to set out on foot again with the children but without him he was worried, but we had proved ourselves able to adapt physically and mentally to the demands of a new environment and way of life.

Where we could go and for how long was limited by time. The nearer the coronation approached, the more rumours flew about: no one would be allowed in or out of the country, the valley, Kathmandu itself, within a month, a week, a few days, of coronation day. No one knew exactly what the restrictions would be, or when they were to be imposed, but already, with several weeks to go, security precautions were beginning to make themselves felt, with streets or whole areas suddenly sealed off and reopened a few hours later. We did not dare be away for too long, in case we were not allowed back into Kathmandu if the rumours became fact.

After much discussion and poring over maps – which were very confusing, distances and place names varying from one map to another – we decided to leave for a week to walk to the Helambu or Helmu Sherpa area north of Kathmandu. We were fortunate that we had been given visas for two months – normally visas were issued only for a fortnight at a time – but needed new trekking permits, so went again to the tourist office, where several other irate would-be trekkers were being refused visa extensions. They were Americans, and had resorted to angry shouting, which is never likely to get anyone anywhere in a country where politeness and good manners may waste time but certainly save tension. We waited patiently, exchanged civilities and namastes with the tourist officer, and left our passports in his care after explaining our wishes and showing him that our visas were in order.

The trekking permits were made out entirely in Devanagri script when we returned next day, but as we were wished good trekking we assumed everything was in order. We engaged one guide cum porter, who was to find a second porter himself, and spoke just enough English for our everyday needs. Neither the guide/porter KV (I have written his name as it was pronounced) nor his mate, Vishnu, had as much to carry as any of the porters on the previous trek, as I had decided that all we needed was one sleeping bag each, an extra one to spread over us if necessary, the clothes we were wearing, in layers – parkas, thick sweaters, thin sweaters, long-sleeved shirts, T shirts – with one change of underwear, socks, shirts, and plimsolls, and a sun hat and woollen hat each. The only other essentials were sunglasses, a basic medical kit, sterilizing tablets and a small water carrier, and camera, film, notebook, pencil, and trekking guide book; but Megan was allowed to take her two comforting stuffed animals, Sweetypies the monkey and Whiskers the rabbit. They were stuffed down the side of Vishnu's basket during the day, and have never been quite the same shape since.

The Helambu area is to the west of one of the few long-distance roads in Nepal, a Chinese-built highway linking Kathmandu to Kodari on the Tibetan border, and incidentally also providing a road link from Delhi to Llasa. We were to travel for a few hours along the road by bus, before continuing on foot.

The bus we were told was ours, and due to leave at 8.30 a.m., did not inspire confidence. Its radiator grill was off, and a frayed and rusty hawser dangled ominously from the front. KV checked and re-checked that it was the right one, before climbing up the rear ladder to the roof to stow our gear. He had made strenuous but unsuccessful attempts not to be parted from it, and kept getting out to make sure it was still there. By the time we eventually left, nearly an hour late, the giant roof rack was stacked with the baskets of an assortment of local people who had somehow managed to squeeze themselves at least two to every place. How all the baskets stayed in place I cannot imagine, as nothing seemed to be tied down. We were the only foreigners on the bus, and the only people to show any surprise at the method of starting the engine: the reason for the hawser became clear when it was attached to the back of a slightly newer-looking bus, and we were towed out into the street, the engine coughing unhappily into life. The hawser was then removed and the radiator grill replaced.

There were numerous halts for police checks, during which the engine was kept running. On each occasion, KV climbed on to the roof and unpacked our luggage from its baskets – no security chances were being taken so near the coronation. The road wound round hairpin bends, the ground often dropping precipitously only a foot or two away. Just after midday, we reached Panchkal, a dusty group of shacks and cafés, where we had curd, rice flakes, and hot curried beans served on tiny enamel plates, before leaving the road on foot along a wide flat "jeepable" track running beside and a little above a river bed. After two river crossings, one over a murky clay bed, the second time on stepping stones in deeper cleaner water, we were again in country where the only way of getting from place to place was on foot. Our progress was slow, as Alistair was complaining that his knee was hurting. "Sahib's knee," we teased, but I wondered whether we were going to be able to complete the circuit that we were planning in a week – about 100 miles, or over ten miles a day.

KV obviously also felt that we were being over-ambitious, and as soon as we were installed in the Tourist Guest House of Bonapati we took out the map and tried to make a reasonable estimate of where we could expect to spend each night. We were determined not to shorten the route we had worked out, in spite of KV's misgivings, so eventually decided that we would have to allow a little longer. We had been joined by a Nepali, a Chetri as he told us proudly, whose English was good enough to be very helpful in the discussion. As we talked, several villagers gathered to add their advice and shake their heads at my irresponsibility, an Englishwoman setting out with three children, one of whom was in their view little more than a baby. More maps were spread out, warnings given about "bad places", and an offer made to deliver a message the next day telling David and the Waterhouses of our change of plan. A letter was written and handed over to a man who was going to Kathmandu, complicated instructions about where it should be delivered were given with much interpreting, but it never arrived.

We were the only guests in a first-floor communal room with one hard wooden bed, where we sat after supper talking with the Chetri, who was the local family planning officer. He told us that family planning was receiving every possible support from the government. In a country where food is scarce, the increased life expectancy which comes with any improvement in medical services puts a severe strain on resources, so it is obvious that limiting the size of families should be considered necessary. More babies and children were surviving, although the figures for infant mortality were still alarmingly high.

I had expected that there would be resistance, on religious or social grounds, to the idea of contraception. Not at all, we were told: the majority of the people accepted the sense of planning their families. In the previous two months, no fewer than 290 men in the area covered by the family planning officer had had vasectomies, and 24,000 women in the area were already on the Pill. The loop and coil were not liked, and tubectomy, the speciality of our friend Dr Kanti Giri, was difficult to arrange in villages because of the lack of facilities. Only one group of people, the Tamangs, did not readily accept the ideas put forward by the family health posts. This, we were told, was because of the custom for men to marry women older than themselves: so the woman's child-bearing years after marriage were already limited, and the man would not wish to undergo a vasectomy because he would want to be sure he could father more children in a possible second marriage, which might be to a woman nearer his own age.

The family planning officer had told us with pride that he was a Chetri: he expected this to impress us with his status, way above that of the local villagers, who were, he informed us, mere Newaris. Many Chetris hold high posts, receive higher education, and more and more often pay only lip service to the traditions and beliefs of their ancestors, but a large number of them are also farmers, in villages where modern ideas are slower to spread, and for them, belief in their heritage is still important and expressed in the old ways, such as the ceremony when a boy becomes a man (at a surprisingly early age) and receives a sacred red thread as a symbol of superiority.

We left Bonapati early the next morning, stopping just outside the village to look at a small family pottery. As there was a plentiful supply of clay in the area, several of these potteries had been established. The clay was grey, a quite different colour from the reddish clay we had seen used in the valley. During the day, the potter (a man – I never saw a woman potter) laid his freshly made pots in rows outside to dry. In the evening, he took most of them inside; a few, mainly the larger ones, designed to store water or grain, were left outside, but covered with straw to protect them from the damp night mist. An open-topped kiln, like a tumbledown barn packed with straw and pots, stood ready to be covered and fired.

The air was warm and pleasant – we were only just over 2,500 feet above sea level, having somehow, imperceptibly, come downhill from Panchkal, itself a few hundred feet lower than Kathmandu, but for the next few days would be walking mainly uphill. For a leisurely hour, we walked along an easy track, crossing the river several times, usually over large stepping stones, which were, at that time of year, no problem. A bridge of two uneven tree trunks over fast-flowing and undoubtedly cold water was more alarming. The children managed this better than I did, being more agile and less nervous of falling into water. My ungainly progress on hands and knees was watched with amusement both by my companions, and by several local people on their way to work in terraced paddy fields.

A man who had stopped to watch asked to look through my camera, which he insisted on pointing at the sky. It took me some minutes to realize that he thought it was a telescope, and even longer to explain that even if it had been he would not have seen the stars in broad daylight. I showed him how to look through the viewfinder at his friends, but had no prints with me to show him the end result. He was obviously very disappointed, and far from convinced about the wonders of photography.

Alistair had regained his trekking legs, and we reached the next village, Malemchi Pul, in less time than we had expected. Vishnu kept offering to carry Megan, and KV was at first convinced that "Baby", as he called her affectionately, could not keep up; but she was determined to be independent, and by the time we stopped they were both telling me proudly, "Baby walk very well." Malemchi Pul, at the junction of two rivers, the Malemchi Khola and the Indrawati Khola, was overshadowed by a new suspension bridge stretched high over a single narrow trading street. The houses, stone-walled with wooden balconies and ground-floor verandahs, were plain and well built. Goat kids wandered in and out of the open doors; one, larger and more adventurous than the others, jumped up on to a first-floor balcony. Many of the houses had resting poles for swifts jutting out a little way under the eaves.

The inhabitants of Malemchi Pul were Tamangs, but as the Tamang people usually live higher in the hills, preferring to farm above 5,000 feet, this settlement must be comparatively recent. In a census done in 1961, about half the Tamangs in the country were living in the hills to the east of the Kathmandu valley, and around a quarter in the western hills. The rest were divided between the valley and the Terai, where they had moved to trade or farm as the country developed. Although all the Tamangs we met spoke Nepali, their own language is nearer to Tibetan, and they are said to have come from Tibet. Before the name Tamang (from Tibetan *ta*, horse, and *mang*, trader) was generally adopted, they were often known as *Bhote*, meaning Tibetan.

Although they are Buddhists, Tamangs observe Dasain, the main Hindu festival, which involves sacrificing and eating goats and chickens. The men who perform the sacrifices are priests, known as *bompo*, and each separate Tamang clan (there are many) has its own bompo. They also have general priests known as *lamas* and considered to be of a superior social rank. Lamas, who officiate at funerals, when cremation and feasting are combined on high places, may and do marry, choosing the daughters of other lamas as their wives; their sons are also brought up to be lamas, and so they have almost become a separate group, and many people call all Tamangs Lama as a term of respect.

In spite of certain taboos, such as never having garlic, nettles, or buffalo meat (which must be cooked outside) in their houses, Tamang customs seem very permissive. No one minds if the girls, or if widows, have babies; premarital affairs are not frowned upon, so long as no sexual relations occur between people from the same clan – this is absolutely forbidden. If a woman goes off with another man, the man pays the equivalent of a few pounds to her husband; a smaller fine is paid to the husband if the wife commits adultery without actually leaving him.

Although arranged marriages are still common among Nepalese people, many groups look favourably on less formal and cheaper ways of marrying. Tamangs may for instance choose their own partners, telling their parents of their decision, and eloping if the parents do not give official consent, or they may try marriage by capture; the boy or man kidnaps his intended bride, but if she still says no after three days he reluctantly lets her go home – a basic and straightforward approach.

Immediately we left the village we began to climb, the scenery changing rapidly the higher we walked. The river valley was fertile and green over its grey clay soil, but soon we were walking over red earth. Deep cracks and crevices showed signs of recent underground upheaval, and it was easy to believe that the rocks of the Himalayan foothills are, as geologists tell us, still young and unstable. The hills rose more steeply and were closer together than in the area near Annapurna. For some time we were out of sight of any houses, then as we approached a solitary small-holding set on a flat fertile platform cut out of a steep slope, a woman came out, carrying a stainless steel dish of bananas from a tree beside the house. I was surprised, as I had always thought bananas were a bonus of the tropics; we were 3,000 feet up, and it was still winter, but the farm was on the sunnier more sheltered side of the hill. The children were all looking hopeful, so I bought a cluster of twenty bananas for three rupees – about three fifths of an English penny each. They were very small, but sweet and firm. We ate one each immediately, telling the woman how delicious they were – "*Dere ramrosha*". She seemed pleased, and we walked on after putting our hands together and taking formal leave.

On several high ridges, we passed small tumbled pyramids of stones, memorials to the dead known as *chorten*. The sky darkened and a biting wind blew from the Himalayan range only a few miles to the north during the afternoon. The chorten on isolated windswept points looked lonely and dramatic. By mid afternoon it had started to rain coldly, and we sheltered in an apparently deserted village of scattered thatched houses. We were planning to reach a Sherpa village, Sermatang, for the night, but by 4 o'clock the rain was heavy, and it was obvious that we would be very wet if we walked for another two hours, the time KV estimated it would take.

Leaving us sheltering under a tree on a narrow rock-tumbled steep path, he went to investigate the possibility of staying in one of the houses scattered over the hillside. A fierce spirit of independence seemed to have decided that each family should build at least a hundred yards from the next. He came back looking worried, saying that he had found a house where we could stay; but, he explained, it was small, the people were poor, and we would have to sleep on an outside balcony. It was, however, the only alternative to walking on in the rain. A thunderstorm was brewing black over the hills, and we could hear the first rumbles of thunder as the rain grew heavier. We had been climbing steadily for six hours, and walking for the best part of eight hours, and were, without having felt it much of an effort, 5,000 feet higher than when we had set out.

We found we were in an area inhabited by yet another racial group – the third that day. The family were Sherpas, and their house was quite different from any we had so far visited. Five people lived together in a first floor room, reached by an outside wooden staircase and across the narrow balcony where we were to sleep. Animals and stores were kept on the ground floor. In the family room, a smoky floor fire gave the only heat and light; by the time the six of us had squeezed in, there was scarcely room for the wife to prepare the food. We sat close together on the floor, making friends with her three children, all scantily clad and suspicious, while she somehow managed to produce enough rice, vegetables, and buffalo milk to satisfy everyone. To warm us while we waited for supper, we were given steaming bowls of Sherpa tea, which I found delicious, and the children thought revolting as it was flavoured with salt and butter instead of sugar and milk; my efforts to reproduce its flavour at home have been greasy failures.

KV had decided that it was his responsibility to make sure Megan was properly nourished, which meant she must eat everything and not live entirely on eggs. There was no cutlery, so we all ate as neatly as we could with the fingers of our right hands, KV squatting beside Megan shoving fingerful after fingerful of food into her mouth. "Eat, baby, eat," he urged each time she hesitated. She was too shy to protest, feeling she might hurt his feelings, and from then on ate everything, however hotly spiced, from his hand. The meal was followed by *tato raxi*, which gave us internal warmth for the night outside. As we squeezed like cold sardines into our sleeping bags on the balcony, we could hear the family inside muttering Buddhist prayers in the dark. It was raining hard, with occasional white flashes of lightning outlining the hills with an eerie clarity; thunder rumbled from hill to hill as we drifted into sleep, fully clothed, keeping even our parkas, gloves and woolly hats on, with our spare sleeping bag stretched across us all. Fortunately, the balcony was shielded by the overhanging eaves and open only to the south and the river valley way below, so that the icy rain and wind coming from the north swept over the roof leaving us dry and relatively cosy.

The storm had passed by morning, but during the night the rain had turned to snow, and we woke to crystal clear cold air as dawn rose over the hills, bathing them in a soft pink misty glow, misty row after distant misty row. From our balcony, we could see back along three valleys and down to three river beds. Crisply powdered snow covered everything on the higher ground. It was the Tibetan Buddhist New Year's Day, and our hosts were droning their morning prayers indoors. Outside their house and each of the other houses scattered down the hillside a new white prayer flag hung limp in the cold still air from its flagpole, a tall stripped pine trunk, white without the bark except for a green tuft left at the top; the tufted tops were spattered with snow. At 6.30, the family gathered outside for yet more prayers, carrying little dishes of embers and incense. As soon as this ceremony was over, we all warmed ourselves by the fire inside, drinking Sherpa tea and eating hot chilli potatoes for breakfast.

12

Tibetan Buddhist New Year

KV and Vishnu started the morning walking barefoot, as they always did, but the snow was cold and uncomfortable even to their tough-skinned feet, so after only a few minutes' steep uphill climb we stopped to unpack our spare plimsolls for them. They seemed as proud of their new footwear as if they had bought themselves the most expensive boots. It was still early when we left, and for an hour and a half we needed to keep moving as energetically as possible, as we were soon on the sunless side of the hill. The ground under scrubby bushy trees was rock-frozen, and in places where the shelter of a conifer had kept the snow away the earth had been crumbled very fine by the frost. By 9 o'clock, we were in the Sherpa village of Sermatang, where we should have spent the previous night. The houses were again well spaced, each with its prayer tree and prayer flag, the roofs and paddy fields a picture postcard winter scene under their powdering of snow.

KV took us to the house of the local lama, where we removed our shoes before going into a warm comfortable room. We were asked not to smoke in the house, the only time we met this restriction. The lama was sitting cross-legged on a carved wooden bed with his back to the only window. In front of him was an array of jars of drink, rice bread, and little dishes of food and spices. The village faithful were paying their respects in endless succession, each bringing a gift and receiving a symbolic tika on the forehead. As he acknowledged the gifts, benevolently blessing the giver with the holy mark, the lama kept up a constant drone of prayers. But he seemed to have a privileged and comfortable existence, living in some style with his wife and three daughters. The carved wooden furniture – a bed, several chests, and shelves lined with gleaming pots and pans – was richer than any we had seen elsewhere. A Buddhist shrine twinkled with the light of several candles – in themselves a sign of wealth – behind yet more dishes of edible offerings.

In honour of the New Year we were given a dish of crisp crunchy apples and rice chapattis. The latter we found heavy and tasteless, but, not wishing to offend, managed to eat one each, slipping the rest surreptitiously into our pockets, where they remained, a soggy mess, for several days. Our offers to pay were refused. "It is the New Year," the lama's daughter told us, "at New Year all are welcome and none must pay." And after all, there seemed no shortage of food, as while we sat chatting and watching for an hour or two more and more local people paid New Year homage to Buddha and his representative.

Eventually we took our leave, continuing in and out round the side of the hill. As we came round the last bend to the far side, where the morning sun had warmed the air and melted some of the snow, we could see both back over the hills we had crossed and forward to the snow-covered mountain peaks, sharply etched against the clear cold blue of the winter sky. It was still cold, with pockets of snow lying in the shadows, as we walked through a forest, but soon we were walking on open ground, and as it became gradually hotter we stripped off our layers of clothing until we wished we could also take off the last layer.

The furthest point of our trek was to be Helambu; but as KV kept telling us we were in Helambu, then saying we would soon reach Helambu where we would spend the night, and varied this by telling us how far it still was to Tarke Ghyang, where we were to sleep, I became very confused. Gradually we worked out what he meant; Helambu, as well as being the name for a Sherpa village, was also the name given to the whole area; while Tarke Ghyang was an alternative name for the village itself. In spite of the sun, there was still enough snow on the terraced roofs and fields ahead of us as we approached Tarke Ghyang to etch the outlines sharply, as we were by this time 9,000 feet above sea level. On the outskirts of the village, at some distance from the main group of houses tightly wedged together in tiers up the hill, a large hotel with traditional wooden frames and eaves stood half built and deserted.

A water-driven prayer wheel in a building like a stone sentry box had been erected over a fast-flowing stream – a very practical way of gaining credit by sending up prayers without even the effort of spinning the wheel. Above it was a new-looking temple and monastery. In front of the temple, on a flat platform, an imposing row of stripped prayer flag trees stood tall and white against a backcloth of mountain peaks and blue sky. Through an open door we could see the temple's main prayer wheel, a recent acquisition twenty feet high and brightly painted – a source of great pride to the lama, at whose house immediately next to the holy buildings we were to stay.

I was again struck by the comfortable life of a lama. The house was in the attractive Sherpa style, L-shaped, with the stable and store room underneath the living, cooking, and sleeping room. Pots of geraniums made a splash of bright colour on the first floor verandah, and wooden steps led up to the short arm of the L, which was used as a wash house and where shoes were left outside the door to the main room. Inside, the long wall facing the door was lined with carved chests and dark wooden dressers, on which gleamed an impressive collection of copper pots, brassware, and gaily decorated enamel plates, as well as an incongruous assortment of empty tins for which all sorts of uses could be found. Everything was spotless.

As at the lama's house in Sermatang, the focal point was a Buddhist shrine, lit by candles; Buddha and the lama had again been brought many offerings. The lama was sitting cross-legged, praying, giving tika and blessings, and accepting offerings from his elevated position on the giant-sized marital bed. He too lived with his family – wife, daughter, son, and grandson, Tashi, a minute four-year-old who was never still for a second. "If I were his mother, I'd chain him to the floor," Alistair commented. Tashi was soon making friends with my children with no inhibitions and none of the apathy or apparent backwardness we had seen in many small Nepali children. His grandmother made us Sherpa tea, shaking it up in a long narrow cylinder as tall as a man, and then pouring it into a modern Thermos flask to keep it hot. Although she spoke no English, we managed to have an amicable sign language conversation with her, careful not to disturb her husband's muttered praying and blessing.

The name Sherpa originally meant people from the east; the best known Sherpa area is Solu Khumbu, under Mount Everest and about a hundred miles east of Helambu. It is through their connections with Everest climbing expeditions that the Sherpas are well known even to people who know little else about Nepal, and many people now refer to all porters and guides in Nepal as Sherpas, or even give the name to all Nepalese people.

Because they have always lived near to the Tibetan border, building villages at altitudes over 10,000 feet up to the highest land which can be cultivated at around 14,000 feet, the Sherpas have of course associated and traded with Tibetans. They speak Tibetan, and wear warm colourful clothing and leather boots like the Tibetans, and follow the Buddhist faith. According to the season, they often move around, grazing their cattle on high slopes in summer and lower slopes in winter, or carrying out different jobs in connection with crops farming at different altitudes. To my surprise, I discovered that their main food was potatoes, rather than rice; rice would not grow so high up, but then nor I had thought would potatoes, which are a fairly recent change from *tsampa*, a solid barley meal which used to be the staple diet and is often still eaten. We were served potatoes several times highly spiced with chilli, and tasting as fresh as English new potatoes – this at the end of their winter.

The Sherpa's beast of burden and provider of milk, butter, and wool is the yak. Yaks, useful, picturesque but stubborn beasts, are used on the higher slopes, but cannot live below 10,000 feet – because of their thick hairy coats, they apparently sweat to death if they come much lower. They are however cross bred with cows, to produce a creature referred to as a dzo; the male crossbreed is a dzopkyo and the female a dzum, and like mules they cannot breed, but are not so pig-headed as yaks, and can be used as beasts of burden and for ploughing. Trading dzos for female yaks (naks) was before the Chinese closure of Tibet a profitable Sherpa trade; the Tibetans were prepared to swop two of their naks for a dzo.

It used to be and probably still is common for two Sherpa brothers to share a wife; if there were three boys in the family, the middle one was enrolled as a monk at an early age, and expected, unlike the lamas, to lead a life of celibacy. There were several young monks at the monastery in Tarke Ghyang. We were exploring the village, wandering through the narrow alleys between long picturesque rows of terraced houses, when a couple of them appointed themselves our exuberant guides. They posed eagerly for photos, then plagued us

KV (centre, holding basket strap) and Vishnu (beside basket) at the start of our second trek; Jane, on the right, was eleven and as tall or taller than both of them

River crossing of stepping stones. In the monsoon the river will flood and become impassable

The monastery at Tarke Ghyang, with Buddhist prayer flags newly erected for the Tibetan New Year

A typical Sherpa house. Alistair is taking his shoes off before going into it. The wicker basket acts as a hen coop

Above: Sherpa village and terracing at 10,000 feet

Below left: Megan, Jane and Alistair in front of the Helambu Hotel at Chiul

Below right: Jane crossing a suspension bridge; the planks are not attached and tend to swing sideways through the gaps at the side

The village of Pati Bhanyang

The two children who watched us suspiciously at Pati Bhanyang

An ox cart near the Indian border at Birganj. Carts are used in the flat Terai in the south

Jane, Alistair and Megan waiting for the bus at Hetauda. They are wearing hand-woven jackets of yak hair bought in Kathmandu

King Birendra (right), about to be crowned after a long ceremony

King Birendra Bir Bikram Shah Dev with Queen Aishwarya Rajya Laxmi Devi Shah on his coronation day

The five-hour coronation ceremony took place in this specially built pavilion in the ancient Hanuman Dhoka palace

The king and queen in the coronation procession

Part of the coronation procession

Civil servants in official costume lining up to pay homage to the king

plaintively and cheekily for "pice". We made the mistake of giving in to their request, and were soon surrounded by a gaggle of children all asking for tips as we wandered round the village with much laughter and backchat in a mixture of pidgin English, Nepali, and Sherpa Tibetan.

The rows of houses up the hillside were so close together that their shadows darkened the paved courtyards between them. The monks and their secular friends guided us to a gate through a high stone wall into a courtyard where a New Year party was in full swing. A triangular paved space between houses was already crowded, but we were welcomed as if we were honoured guests whose arrival had been eagerly awaited. The women and girls were wearing their gayest clothes, heavily laden with necklaces and ornamental belts. Most of the people were sitting on the ground, eating rice chapattis and drinking a sort of alcoholic butter tea. This tasted like and was as strong as rakshi, but with the addition of the grease and spice of the Sherpa tea, and was best drunk quickly while it was still too hot for the grease to congeal. It was poured liberally from a teapot into glasses, and seemed already to have had some effect on the merry line of villagers queuing up in front of a lama sitting with several attendants just inside the gate. We were persuaded to join the queue – the fact that we did not share the local beliefs and were confused about what was expected seeming to have no importance. To refuse the hospitality of blessing so warmly extended to us as complete strangers would have seemed churlish and unfriendly, especially as we had accepted food and drink.

We watched the people in front of us carefully to see what we should do in this informal outdoor Buddhist communion ceremony, before kneeling in turn before the lama, heads bent and hands pressed together. A teaspoonful of fine flour and sugar from a row of little dishes was put between our lips, like uncooked communion wafer, then, our hands piously joined finger to palm, we received the tika on our hair – three large blobs of grease which soon melted unpleasantly. Finally, we had to make a financial contribution (to Buddha or the lama, I wondered) before making obeisance, hands still pressed together, first to the lama, then to his helpers, then to the assembled company, who had been watching curiously to see how we would acquit ourselves. We seemed to have passed the test, as immediately more rice chapattis and full glasses of steaming buttery alcohol were pressed upon us.

Back at our host lama's house, supper was ready. As soon as we had eaten, the lama, his religious duties for the day over, turned to more secular matters: with limited English, he embarked on an unequalled sales patter, asking us £25 for a huge heavy neck ornament. He claimed that it was of unsurpassed antiquity and value, the most sought after bargain; that only for us would he part with it especially so cheaply; and that as we were English we must be rich, and what was £25 to us? I could honestly assure him that I did not have that much money on me. He was persistent and persuasive, and resumed his efforts the next morning before we left; but it was all with the greatest good humour, and no doubt it was not too long before someone richer and more gullible turned up.

After supper, we returned to the party; by this time food and drink had obviously been consumed in some quantity. A form of swaying dancing had started, the dancers, men, women, and children, linking arms round each other's shoulders and waists in a line, surrounding those still sitting on the ground. Jane and Alistair were drawn into the circle and were soon part of the monotonous rhythmical movement from side to side. The young monks spotted us across the courtyard, and made friendly advances to Megan, who although seven years younger looked as old as they did. While we watched the sleepy half intoxicated dancing, their attentions became more and more friendly, and by the time Jane and Alistair rejoined us they were stroking her arms and hands in a most unmonklike way.

A dark-eyed rosy-cheeked woman wanted to know where my husband was; that I was travelling without him with the children aroused interest and curiosity everywhere. We were joined by an inebriated young man who felt that it was time Jane and Alistair were paired off with a young Sherpa boy and girl. In his eyes, they were both of an age to indulge in an amorous adventure, or even be married. I decided that things were beginning to get out of hand, and we said goodbye all round before the good-humoured friendliness had degenerated. "Weren't the monks kind and friendly, Mummy?" Megan said innocently as we left.

The lama and his wife were already asleep in the big double bed. A young man, their son or son-in-law, was sitting up in a second bed facing the door, intoning his prayers from a great flat book. KV and Vishnu were sitting on the floor chatting quietly by the embers of the fire. This communal sleeping, with several people of different sexes and ages all sharing the only room, seemed to cause no embarrassment to anyone. Being an inhibited westerner, I often wondered what they did about sex – there was never any nocturnal sexual activity that I was aware of in any house we stayed in. When and where did they do it?

When we woke in the morning, the young man was already praying again, swaying slightly, wearing a long white shirt – or perhaps he had continued all night. The fire was lit and the lama and his wife up well before seven. The ground was still frozen when we left, and the air bitterly cold as the sun had not crept round the hill. Not far from the village, we met a group of men resting on a bussoni. They had already chopped enough wood to fill their baskets, which were in a row on the stone platform. I tried to lift one, and even with help could not stagger more than a step or two; yet they thought nothing of walking many miles, up and down the mountainside, carrying these great loads. It is no wonder that many people die young from heart strain. Beside the bussoni and its spreading shade tree was a line of chorten, built on a promontory overlooking the valley, and a small unadorned stone temple.

By the time we stopped for breakfast and lunch combined, we had walked down and then up the equivalent of an English mountain; but we did not feel any great sense of achievement, as by this time we were all so used to it that we often forgot to ask KV how far we would have to climb before the next stop, or how many hours walk away the next meal was. Even Megan, who had complained at times on the first trek, was having no problems keeping up, and KV's initial apprehension had changed to friendly pride.

The L-shaped Sherpa house we stopped at could almost have been an isolated Cotswold stone farmhouse, with bright pots of geraniums on the steps and at the door and window. A dog rushed out to bark as we approached it past a magnolia tree in full flower. A girl was dispatched to buy eggs for us from a neighbour; another came back from a water fetching excursion carrying an enormous full crock. KV and Vishnu were in no hurry to leave, as they were soon happily drinking great glassfuls of strong bitter chang. By the time we started walking again, it was midday, and the sun was hotter than we had known it. Our path, alternately soft and sandy or loose and shaly, led through what was once a forest; but generations of tree cutting for fuel and fodder had left little more than stunted mis-shapen bushes. Soon we were longing for shade as the path plunged steeply down to a suspension bridge, slung alarmingly high over rocky fast flowing water.

To our relief, KV decided that it would be better for us to walk along the river bed rather than cross the bridge to a higher path. Although when I think of a suspension bridge, I picture a strong modern construction inspiring confidence, this particular bridge looked far from safe. True, it was suspended – but was merely a row of wobbly single planks between chain hand rails. The water far below looked uninviting as it swirled round the boulders of the river bed. It was peaceful as we picked our way over rocks, the only sound the soothing rushing of the water, which was caught in eddies by gleams of sunlight.

We were no longer in Sherpa country as we climbed from the river to the village at Chiul; the contrast between the neatness and cleanness of the Sherpa villages and the higgledly-piggledly scruffiness of Chiul reminded me of crossing the Swiss border into France. Although the house where we were to stay called itself grandly Helambu Hotel, it was unlike any hotel I had seen – a dilapidated little two-storey square stone building, where we shared the one small downstairs room with a goat, two dozen hens, and a couple of children. It was a busy place; all evening, local people popped in to chat, have a drink, and inspect the latest eccentric trekkers. Shortly after dark, there was a violent thunderstorm, and more people scurried in for shelter. We watched the lightning against the opposite hill, glad that we were on the ground floor, as the hotel roof looked none too rainproof. The storm moved away as suddenly as it had come; the goat was chained in a corner and the hens shut into a hole under the stairs for the night. By the time we had spread our sleeping bags out, there was scarcely room for the adult occupants to reach the stairs to go up to their own quarters. The two Nepali children were working out some mathematical homework problem by the glimmer of one wick lamp as we started a battle with fleas in our sleeping bags.

While we were paying our bill in the morning, KV and the hotel owner were talking rapidly together, both pointing excitedly in different directions. KV was looking worried, and told us that we could not walk along the river as we had planned; it was, he had been assured, far too dangerous, a haunt of robbers, who might jump out at us from behind rocks. The bank was hidden from view by steeply rising hills, so no one would be able to come to our aid. I was prepared to take the risk, confident that the local people would be as friendly, gentle, and courteous as usual; but KV refused adamantly, saying he would not take the responsibility and obviously frightened.

So, inwardly cursing the landlord, as we would have to walk and climb much further, we set out along a hillside path to the next suspension bridge. When we saw this bridge, which made the one we had avoided the previous day look almost inviting, I felt it would have been far better to face bandits than risk our lives by crossing. Twice the length of the bridge we had avoided, it was far higher above the water. The gaps between the bent and rusted bars linking its planks to the handrail were big enough for an elephant to fall through; and the handrails themselves were so far apart that I could only just reach them by stretching and Jane and Alistair only with their finger tips. Even KV and Vishnu were alarmed, and gave strict instructions that only one person must cross at a time, as the swaying motion started by even the slowest walk sent the row of single planks, loosely laid end to end, veering wildly from side to side. Vishnu went first, with his basket of our belongings; he returned for Megan, who could not possibly walk across herself, as there was nothing for her to hold on to. She was told to get on his back, hold on tight like a baby monkey, and keep absolutely still as if she moved it would throw them both off balance.

I watched until she was on the other side; then it was Jane's turn, followed as soon as she was safe by Alistair. "Slowly, slowly," as KV had told them, they edged forwards, eyes all the time on the far bank. When it came to my turn, nothing but sheer necessity and their example urged me away from the edge. I did not dare look down at the swirling rock-strewn water.

The scenery the other side of the river as we followed a comfortably wide grassy track was softer, the hills less abrupt and more undulating, than in the Helambu area. At the village of Chiera, a busy place with a row of shops, one stacked with bales of cloth, we bought six foot lengths of sugar cane, freshly cut by hand, and chewed and spat contentedly for the rest of the day as we walked. Sugar cane grows only on the lower slopes and valleys, so we must have come down further than we had realized.

Banana and fig trees, and a variety of flowering cherries not yet in bloom, grew on rich red soil. We could almost imagine ourselves for a while in an English wood, but for the birds – long-tailed birds showing bright flashes of colour as they flew from tree to tree, small bright yellow and black or red and black birds, and dozens of white paddy birds sitting like miniature storks on the fields, which were irrigated by little hand-cut channels diverting the water from the river and streams.

The fertile well-watered country continued along the valley to Patechour, another prosperous looking village with shops. In both Patechour and Chiera, several new houses had been built of highly prized but ugly concrete, with shaped tiles on the roofs. A large and pretentiously designed new school was half built, again using concrete, incongruous beside the older houses. The water from the river was being used to power several mills, including one alongside a two-storey house with a mill wheel reaching to the eaves. Patechour was obviously a flourishing place, but we soon left its tall trees behind and were again on a bare harsh hillside.

Our next stopping place was Taramarang, picturesque, lively, and scruffy. We scrambled down a steep path to the junction of two rivers, the hillside towering oppressively over a row of terraced shops and houses built just high enough above the monsoon water level to avoid flooding. At the river end of the village, food was being served from two rush huts which looked unhygienic and uninviting, and which KV decided were not suitable places for us to eat. He took us to one of the houses along the street, where we sat on a first floor balcony overlooking people and gaudy cockerels in the dust. An English vegetarian restaurant owner from London joined us, asking where we had been; he had turned back as the soles of his shoes had worn through, and the children were delighted to tell him about the Sherpa villages further away.

Before we left Taramarang, over another wobbly bridge, KV bought some rice, as he was not sure where we would find food that evening. I suggested we should stop for the night in a village called

Takani, which looked from the map conveniently placed; but KV said it was a "bad village"; and once he had made up his mind, as we had already learnt, nothing would change it. We could see Takani as we walked along a hill ridge path; it looked cheerful and safe, with New Year celebrations in progress, coloured prayer flags flying and several bonfires burning. A crowd of gaily dressed people had gathered in front of two mat huts, and the sound of drums drifted up to us. On a hill overlooking the village was a long white monastery building, and I next tried to persuade KV to go there for the night, having heard of warm hospitality to guests in Buddhist monasteries. But "bad place" he insisted.

As a rich red sunset over the Kathmandu valley began to cast long evening shadows, we were on a narrow shaly path, at times barely passable because a recent landslide had taken much of the side of the hill with it. The shale was so loose and the path so steep, sloping away over a tumbled nearly sheer drop, that KV was worried we would slip; so, I must confess, was I, as at times there was only just enough room to pick our way along a track scratched across a cliff face. By the time we reached a wide cropped grass clearing, where a solitary stone house stood beside a stagnant pool, it was almost dark.

Fortunately we were able to stay at this house, but would have to provide our own food. KV and Vishnu would not (to my relief) hear of allowing me to cook, and took $2\frac{1}{2}$ laborious hours to produce ample rice but little else. While they were busy blowing the fire into reluctant life, we stood on a ridge admiring the last glow of sunset against hills and mountains stretching to and beyond the Kathmandu valley in swiftly darkening rows.

Our hosts were two Tamang bachelors. All they had in their house, one room 10 feet by 15 feet, was a stack of wood for the fire, a couple of sacks of stores, and a few plates, glasses, and cooking pots. It was just high enough for me to stand up – when I jumped up rather too quickly, I hit my head hard on the stone ceiling.

Dawn over the mountains was as spectacular as the previous evening's sunset, and although there was a bite in the early morning air we stood admiring the scenery from a windswept vantage point on short springy grass before walking on along a path as narrow as the one approaching the house, again above an almost sheer drop. In the hour it took us to reach Pati Bhanyang, an official police check post, the scenery had again changed dramatically. A young man, scarcely more than a boy, was in charge of the joint village shop and hotel. His English, which he had learnt from tourists, was good; he told us that both his parents were working in Kathmandu, where two married sisters also lived with their husbands. Another brother – there were seven children in the family – had recently moved to the city, but he had no wish to follow him. The family was obviously fairly wealthy, owning both the shop house and another house opposite, which had been rented to the police. Both houses were large and elegantly proportioned, with an air of importance and distinction.

Although we had expected to have to show them our passes, the police showed no interest in us, being far too busy playing cards in the sun, but when I stood in the shop porch to take a photo, they leapt to their feet with shouts and gesticulations as the cards were hastily hidden from sight. "They don't want you to take their picture," the young shopkeeper explained. "They are not smart and are not working hard. Someone might see it." As it was the only place from which I could take a general shot of the village, an attractive huddle of roofs against smoky hills, I was unwilling to give in, so asked him to tell them that I would photograph only the rest of the village, leaving them out. "Tell her to bugger off," I could imagine them saying, as protests and explanations were shouted back and forth with some ill will. Eventually, the sensitive officials were persuaded that I was not a spy from the city, goodwill was restored, and a photo taken (without police).

While KV and Vishnu cooked rice, dahl, and fried potatoes under a long verandah at the back of the house, we watched everything around us, explored, and talked to the occupants. Grandmother was busy at her puja, going from shrine to shrine, carrying candles and dishes of incense, ringing a hand bell, and intoning endless prayers. One shrine, to which she returned several times, was under trees behind the house and another inside the house, with a large permanent bell. We were worried we might offend or disturb her, but she stopped in her devotions to talk and explain her actions in a combination of odd English words and Nepali. She had no objection to posing for a photo, and led us to the open door in front of the house shrine, dedicated to Vishnu.

The rest of the spacious ground floor area of the house, apart from the shop, rear verandah and shrine, served as stables. Three buffalo, two cows, and two calves were let out to eat a heap of dried bamboo leaves. Several women were washing clothes, fetching buckets of water from a spring beside the outdoor shrine, and taking no notice of the animals wandering about among them. When they had finished the laundry, draping it on bushes to dry, they washed their hair, hanging their heads forward so that they could slap it dry in the sun. Bees from log hives on the wall near the stable door were busy in the late winter warmth. We managed to discover, with much buzzing, sign language and counting on fingers, that each hive gave about 15 pounds of honey in a good year – half what we would expect from our bees on average. While we watched everyone else, two shy little girls watched us, gradually venturing nearer and nearer.

Although we were not far from the valley, we found we still had to climb before starting the final descent. At first we were on a steep sandy track, with high banks, like a medieval Cornish lane; then on high ground over a double-hummocked hill known as Burlang Bhanyang Pass. After an hour in forest, we stopped in the scattered village of Chaubas, where the only available refreshment was rakshi; women like walking haystacks passed us, bent under their loads until their backs were not far from horizontal; most of the menfolk seemed to be sitting outside doing nothing.

For several miles, or an hour and a half after Chaubas, the path was as flat as any in the Nepalese hills; and then, suddenly, we came round a bend out of the forest, starting going down, and there was the Kathmandu valley, the city itself and to its left the airport, way below us. In a scattered Tamang village on the grassy hillside, the influence of commercialism was obvious. A woman carrying a baby in a shawl on her back asked for money in return for posing for a photo; another came wheedling and begging; a man and then a woman appeared from their house to ask for cigarettes; several children followed us, alternately demanding pice and a smoke. There was neither kindliness nor goodwill in these demands.

KV took an instant dislike to both the people and the place, and when he learnt that we would be charged thirty rupees for floor space in a dirty dilapidated house, decided that this was yet another "bad village", and that we would try to find accommodation further down the hill, if necessary walking right down to the valley and returning to

Kathmandu in the dark. To our relief, we were made welcome at the last house in the village, a fine spacious two-storey wooden building, with a balcony and verandah running along two sides and a neatly thatched roof. The owner and his family had built it entirely themselves, but it was not quite finished, he told us; he still had to make some built-in furniture and put the final touches to the exterior. He was proud of his work, and we were able to tell him warmly how impressed we were (particularly as David is the complete un-handyman).

Inside, the ground floor was one big unfurnished room, with a fire burning at either end. At the far fire, a group of Nepalese guests were preparing their food. The owner's wife was busy cooking for her own family at the other end, welcomed us warmly, and immediately poured out black tea for everyone, apologizing that the day's milk was finished. A row of huge clay water pots stood along one wall; everything was spotless and orderly, and soon we were given supper, which we ate with our fingers. There was no cutlery, our hosts explained, because they had not yet managed to save enough to buy extras. The food was excellent: dark curried dahl, rice as usual, and strips of tender delicious dried chicken.

Megan found the dahl very hot, and to my horror KV, who was still feeding her by hand at every meal, reached for the communal water pot to give her a drink. Before I could stop him, he had poured the water between her lips, her attempt to protest cut short by the necessity of swallowing or choking. "What shall I do?" she asked me in a whisper, as not drinking the water had been a strictly enforced rule while trekking, or indeed anywhere in the country; although the local people can drink it with no apparent ill effect, it was a risk we had to be careful not to take. "Never mind – we're nearly back now; you've already had some, so if you're thirsty you'd better drink," I said. At least, I thought, we would soon be back in Kathmandu and near a doctor if necessary; but she suffered no ill effects.

In this house it was impossible not to be aware of the contrast between the old ways of the villages and the introduction in the valley of new ideas and technology. We were a few hours' walk from the city, not far above the hydro-electric station and reservoir providing power and water to the people of the valley; but the only light in the house came from two tiny wick lamps, and water was fetched from a spring. Below us after dark, the runway of the airport linking the country with the rest of the world was clearly outlined, and we could hear and see the jets; yet when I asked to take a photo of the wife with her small daughter, so that I could remember their friendliness and hospitality, she covered both their faces and turned away in fear.

By six next morning, the fire was lit and work had started, and by the time we were fully awake, the husband was chipping away at some wood for a door or window frame; his only tools, with which the whole house had been built, were kukris and axes and the little paring knives which go with the kukris. A girl was stripping greens, a woman was weaving a basket, another cooking at the fire. The sleeping mats of the other guests were already rolled up and the floor swept. Some kind of grain was being shaken clean on a circular winnowing mat. We felt very lazy, still in our sleeping bags in the midst of all this activity, and did not like to interrupt the work to ask for tea, as we knew that the first work break and meal, as usual in Nepalese farming communities, would not be until mid morning, so as soon as we were dressed we said goodbye and started on our last downhill walk, past Sundrijal dam, water works, and power station, and on to a long flat straight valley road.

Now and then a cluster of trees broke the monotony of flat paddy fields; an occasional car or bicycle clattered past, and a few minutes of diversion were caused by the discovery of some European-style beehives similar to our own. The valley, cut in places by sudden flat-topped hills which looked as if they had been levelled by a mighty swipe of a giant's, or perhaps god's, kukri, was totally enclosed by hills and mountains.

We had begun to lose interest in walking by the time we stopped for our first food of the day opposite an impressive temple, the temple of Gokarno. Dedicated to Shiva, in the Nepalese month of Bhadra it is a place of pilgrimage and puja, in honour of dead fathers. We were not, frustratingly, allowed to see behind the elaborate closed gilt doors, although some kind of ceremony was obviously in progress. Outside, holy water was being liberally sprinkled and gifts to the gods offered at a shrine; and at several nearby exotic but dilapidated shrines, smaller temples, and wash places, people were worshipping with offerings, more holy water and prayers. The main temple was in a reasonably good state of repair, but the other buildings had been allowed to fall into a sad state and were disfigured by those symbols of modern development, telegraph poles and electricity cables.

From Gokarno, it was a long boring hour's walk in hot sun to Bodnath, where we gave up walking and made the mistake of squeezing into an overcrowded and airless minibus. KV and Vishnu left us at the Waterhouses', after many sad namastes; they kissed our hands and seemed as sorry to go as we were to say goodbye. Vishnu had spoken little during the week, but we had felt that he was sympathetic and that both he and KV, with whom we had talked as much as the limitations of language had allowed, had enjoyed our company as much as we had enjoyed theirs. Perhaps to them we were just another foreign responsibility and brief source of income; but I like to think they remember us, and probably in particular Megan, with the same affection that we remember them. We gave them each a tip which they seemed to feel was generous and which was the most practical way we could think of thanking them. Although we had paid them more than the price originally agreed, the whole week had cost us only £10, including food.

A letter from David's father was waiting for us, enclosing a cutting from the *Daily Telegraph*, which described a trek in the grand style. The writer told proudly how he had enjoyed beautiful mountain scenery and the achievement of walking from place to place without ever setting foot in a Nepalese house. His porters had erected his tent, cooked his food, and arranged for him to walk from a late breakfast until early afternoon, with a stop for lunch thrown in. I felt sorry for him for what he had missed – to us, the walking was healthy, enjoyable and essential to get to the next meal; but the chief pleasure had come from our contact with the people and brief insight into their lives. At the same time, I was angered by his patronizing attitude. As far as I was concerned, the scenery was an appreciated bonus; for the children, who had completed a round trip of about a hundred miles in a week without the food and comfort they were used to at home, I hoped that a long-lasting tolerance and understanding had grown as we walked. The scenery – yes, no one could fail to be moved by it; but moved chiefly by its effect on daily life, by the hard work and endurance it imposed which made any problems we might have at home seem insignificant in comparison with the struggle for basic self-sufficiency and survival.

13

The Terai and the Raj Path

It is difficult to avoid clichés when talking of Nepal; to call it a land of contrasts sounds corny – but is true. We had walked in the Himalayan foothills, seen the towering snow-covered inhospitable peaks, visited hill villages and valley temples, explored Kathmandu and the neighbouring towns, but so far seen nothing of the south, the flat hot low-lying Terai. This region is as great a contrast to the north Himalayas as one could find, yet the two are nowhere separated by more than one hundred miles. Until recently, the Terai was as effective a natural barrier as the mountains, with its malarial jungle, the haunt of tigers, inhabited only by a few hardy tribal groups.

The mosquito has been all but eradicated; jungle has been cleared and in its place is flat fertile farmland, producing enough surplus food for some to be exported to India. Big game hunting expeditions, the favourite pastime of both Shah and Rana rulers, are a memory of the past. Tourists are invited to spend large sums of money and see the remaining wild animals at Tiger Tops, a safari hotel well patronized by American ladies, in the middle of the country's one game park, the Mahendra National Park; guests may take photos of, but not shoot at, rhinos, tigers, elephants and lions, provided the staff have managed to lure them into a suitable position.

David visited Tiger Tops, to film its artificially preserved game and wealthy tourists. I decided to visit a less exotic part of the Terai, Birganj, on the border with India, with the children. There were two reasons for this choice – I felt we had a very incomplete picture of the country if we had seen nothing of the south; and there happened to be a flight leaving for Simra with a bus link to Birganj, with just time to go there and back for a couple of days before the valley was sealed for the coronation. "You must confirm the return flight in Birganj," we were told after paying for the tickets, "there will certainly be no problem."

We took off from Kathmandu in a small plane with a dozen other passengers, climbed rapidly from 4,000 feet to clear the 9,000-foot Mahabharat Mountains to the south of the valley, and immediately started the descent to Simra airstrip at 400 feet – all in fifteen ear-popping minutes. The plane stayed on Simra's bumpy grass airfield for just long enough to take on a full load of twenty passengers. As its wheels cleared the ground, the runway had already reverted to its alternative use as a footpath.

A few of the passengers were met by chauffeur-driven limousines. The rest of us took a bus to Birganj along a straight road between endlessly flat subdivided fields. A single-track railway line, the only one in Nepal, ran parallel to the road twenty miles into the country from India, but was overgrown with grass and had obviously not been used for many years, although Indian trains still travel to Raxaul, just across the border. At frequent intervals, arches of red cloth and paper across the road wished the king long life and health in his reign.

The Terai has a hot humid tropical climate. It was a dull overcast day; a sticky muggy heat was heavy and oppressive, and the colours of the landscape dry and dusty. Birganj looked more Indian than Nepalese, with swarthier-skinned people, many with beards; the more northerly Nepalese people rarely seem to grow enough beard to make shaving more than a weekly necessity. The people of the Terai are a mixture, some the remaining hardy jungle and swamp people, some the farmers and businessmen who have moved south with the growth of agricultural and commercial opportunities; others are of Indian origin, and have either moved north or have always lived on either side of the border.

As soon as we left the bus, we went to the Birganj Tourist Information Office to ask where we should confirm our return flight. The government official sitting in shabby grandeur at a huge desk was surprised but delighted that we had bothered to visit Birganj, and inclined to spend as long as we could spare practising his English. He told us disdainfully that most of the local people belonged to a Terai tribal group, implying that he, as a Newari, was socially far superior, as were the other minority groups of Brahmans, Chetris, and Gurungs who had moved south.

Eventually, the conversation returned to our original question about the flight. He was doubtful about the existence of any such flight, but said we must go to the RNAC (Royal Nepalese Airline Corporation) office, coming out into the street to show us the way, and adding helpfully that he thought it was closed. It was. While we waited for it to re-open we explored the town. It was cattle market day; several enormous bullocks were crammed together in a small enclosure, and a group of men were leaning on the fence making the sort of comments made by farmers at all cattle markets. The women in the street were dressed, Indian style, in full saris, rather than in the half saris or long skirts and cummerbunds of the women in the hill villages. Half a dozen women on a street corner were wailing loudly, the loose ends of their saris pulled over their heads. Children were crowding round a fairground, where stalls and a few roundabouts were being set up for a coronation fête.

We walked down the main street to the edge of the town, within sight of the border. Little shops on stilts lined the road – many houses in the Terai are raised off the ground to prevent flooding when the monsoon rains sweep across the flat plains. There were fewer people on foot than in either the valley towns or the hill villages; carts, some covered, drawn by ponies or bullocks, loaded with children, whole families, or merchandise, outnumbered cars and lorries.

At the children's insistence, we hired two tricycle rickshaws for an hour. With Alistair and Jane on one, and Megan and me on the other, our drivers raced each other along the main street, and then down a side street; there were not many turnings to choose from, and soon we had been pedalled wildly along every street in the town. Finally, we were taken past the bus station and out of the town to a water tower and large walled enclosure which we gathered was the local stadium. A crowd had assembled, sitting on the tops of the high walls and thronging round the outside to cheer on the local sport.

This was pony cart and rickshaw racing. Carts looking like miniature wild west wagons and pulled by skinny little ponies careered round and round the arena, wheels wobbling precariously. At the finish of each race, the winning driver charged out of the arena and continued at full gallop down the street. Pedestrians had a choice of jumping aside or being run down. Almost the entire local population seemed to have gathered to watch, cheer, and no doubt put a few rupees on the favourites.

Leaving the races before the finals, to avoid the crowds, we asked our drivers to take us to the airline office. Alarmingly, they denied its existence; but when they eventually realized I meant the "plane office", they were delighted to point out my stupid mistake. When we climbed down from our elevated position over the back wheels of the tricycles, we were asked what seemed a very reasonable price for the entertainment. I paid in Nepalese rupees; no, no, I was told, you must pay in Indian rupees – which, with five fewer to the pound, were worth more. I was searching for change to make up the difference, when a heated argument broke out around us.

An onlooker explained that another rickshaw driver felt we were being overcharged; I was quite happy to pay what had been asked, I said; but this would not do. By this time a crowd had gathered, and sides were being taken, the intervening drivers feeling that it was a matter of principle to protect me from this unscrupulous extortion of a few extra rupees. We were soon forgotten in the enthusiasm of the argument, and slipped away, leaving the group of drivers shouting and gesticulating.

The airline office was open by this time, but when we presented our tickets we were told regretfully, politely, but firmly, that no reservations had been received; and in any case there was no return flight before the coronation. Worse than this followed – as we had bought our tickets in Kathmandu, and the office there had not passed on our booking, we could not be given a refund in Birganj. I explained, several times, that without the refund we did not have enough money to get back to Kathmandu. Eventually, I managed to persuade the concerned official (a phrase much used in the *Rising Nepal*, the English-language newspaper) that we really had paid for the tickets and that RNAC would not lose by giving us back the cost of the non-existent return flight.

As soon as we had received the refund, we went to the bus station. My suggestion that we should walk back to Kathmandu – which would have taken two or three days – was met with tears from Megan, who found the sunless sticky heat tiring. Even on this dull winter day the temperature must have been well into the 80s. If I had been on my own, or with another adult, I would probably have tried to hitch-hike; but I rejected this idea as irresponsible with children, as the only possible lift would have been perched on top of an open lorry. The bus was therefore the only answer, and as we felt we had seen all there was to see in Birganj, I decided to break the journey by going part of the way that evening and spending the night at Hetauda (or Hitaura, or Hitauda, or Hetaura, depending on the choice of map) thirty miles nearer Kathmandu.

Buying bus tickets was a long and involved process. I had to give all our full names, ages, dates of birth; a complicated discussion followed about which seats would be best for the children, all seats being bookable in advance. Eventually, for just under £5 total cost, we were given tickets to Hetauda for that day, with reservations for the morning bus to Kathmandu. Each ticket had the seat and bus number on it, and the places would definitely be reserved. The bus in the morning was scheduled to leave at 9.30, or perhaps 10.00, but we were advised to wait from 8.30 onwards just in case it was early.

The evening bus, a modern streamlined coach with tinted windows to cut out the glare from the sun, left on time at 5 o'clock. The numbered seat system worked well at first but by 6 o'clock, the time we had expected to arrive in Hetauda, we were only two miles from Birganj and the bus was crowded and stuffy with extra passengers travelling a few stops home from work with their baskets, hens, and small children. Shanty shops, some on stilts, were being closed for the night, while bullock carts, herds of bullocks, and even an occasional elephant, were being led or driven along the flat road. We saw several litters, each carrying two people decked with flowers, on their way to a little temple a few miles from Birganj where a crowd had already gathered in litters, rickshaws and pony carts. As we passed, two elephants arrived, each carrying four or five passengers and decorated with flowers.

Looking back towards India across the seemingly endless flatness, we saw the sun for the first time that day as it vanished in a rich deep-red glow, and the temperature dropped to a pleasant evening warmth. By this time, the bus had already stopped several times to take on or disgorge unbooked passengers. An hour and a half after leaving Birganj, the bus was held up for nearly an hour at a police check point, where I had to show our passports, and give our dates of birth and ages all over again. A peanut vendor walked up and down inside the bus selling his wares while the police asked passengers, none too politely, to turn out their possessions on the floor, paying particular attention to those of Indian appearance, the majority, who were all travelling overnight to Kathmandu. Security had been tightened because of a fear of political demonstrations at the coronation; as Nepalese dissidents and illegal political groups have been known to gather in India, anyone coming from India was suspect.

After the police check, we continued through the forest and hills of the Inner Terai. Although we crossed ten or more river bridges and were aware of steep cliffs and dense trees beside the road, it was too dark to see anything clearly. After another police check, and then a third, both mercifully brief and cursory, although each time I had again to give my age and date of birth, we saw the lights of Hetauda twinkling ahead of us. There is electricity in the southern towns of Nepal, and strings of coloured lights on some of the roofs gave Hetauda a festive look. Naked bulbs in unshuttered rooms threw circles of sharp white light into the night.

The hour's journey had stretched to 3½ hours by the time the bus stopped in the town centre; it was pitch dark, we were hungry, and we had nowhere to stay. The Raj Hotel, a plain solid establishment, soon solved these problems; two clean rooms over the street, each with twin beds and its own lavatory, shower, and basin, cost us a total of thirty rupees (£1.20 – 60p a room, or 30p a bed). We were joined at supper, for which there was a choice of Nepalese or English food, by a lonely German technologist (his description) from the Wuppertal, who made the Raj his base whenever he could escape for a few days from his isolated research project in the forest. He had been in Nepal for three months, and was, to my surprise, being paid by the Nepalese government at German rates.

The cockerels and early morning light woke us at six, and by seven we had had breakfast, paid our bill, and left to explore before waiting for the bus. Compared with Birganj, Hetauda was busy, cheerful and clean, with one main street behind which a small industrial area merged with open farmland. The development of several small factories had brought jobs and comparative prosperity. Behind the factories, thatched single-storey farmhouses were dotted over a slope leading to a wide almost empty river bed. An irrigation channel had been dug out, and over its clear water there were several miniature mills, like the mills over the mountain streams.

By 8.30, we were waiting for our bus on a bench in front of shops which had already been open for some time. By ten o'clock, the bus still had not arrived, and I was beginning to be worried; but was reassured by an army major who spoke enough English to tell us that yes, we were in the right place, no the bus had not passed us, and suggested that we should show our reservations at the ticket office, a small room packed, as was the street outside, with people waiting patiently – families, mothers and babies, with baskets of hens, bundles of belongings and bedding rolls – all unconcerned at the delay. At ten past ten, a bus came in; we showed our tickets – wrong bus; ours was just coming. Two more buses stopped – again, they did not have the number shown on our tickets. To while away the time, I bought some little yellow bananas for two rupees a dozen from a display set out invitingly under a big black umbrella on the pavement. Remembering the flavour of the bananas we had bought when we were trekking, we each unpeeled one in anticipation. I wondered why our purchase had caused merriment among a crowd of children who had inevitably gathered round; and discovered as soon as I bit into my banana – it was bitter and hard, leaving a sour taste in my mouth and shrivelling my palate. Cooking bananas, we were told – it was not yet the season for eating bananas.

By eleven o'clock, I was wondering if we should try hitch-hiking on one of the gaily painted lorries which occasionally rumbled past, displaying the request to "HORN PLEASE" in elaborate letters on their rears. Someone told us our bus had already left – but how, when we had not moved from our place and had looked anxiously at each bus as it drew in, only to be told by the driver that it was not the right one?

By this time, the major, the men in the booking office, and the families sitting among their belongings on the pavement, were all showing active and sympathetic interest in the non-appearance of our bus. On our behalf, lengthy discussions were held with the next few drivers to stop for passengers. Then the booking officer rushed us up to a bus which did not have our number, and was already full. After some talk and waving of hands and looking at watches, the conductor started moving his passengers up to make room for us. This meant that the people occupying the seats we were given had to sit on little wooden benches in the gangway – every bus seemed to have several of these extra places tucked away somewhere. As we were taking seats which had been booked by their occupants in advance, I felt embarrassed at the memsahib-like treatment we were being given, and protested that we were the ones who ought to travel in discomfort. No, no, it would not do for an Englishwoman and her children to sit in the gangway, we must have seats – the other people were used to it, we were told, I must admit to my secret relief. The prolonged discussion the previous day about which seats I should book for the children seemed rather irrelevant by this time, although kindly meant. A passenger from the previous day's flight to Simra was also on the bus, and greeted us warmly like long-lost friends. He too had booked a return flight on the non-existent plane.

One of the men whose place had been taken for our benefit was a quiet gentle Indian wearing a long white draped Indian-style skirt and carrying a battered leather brief case. In the next hour and a quarter, the bus stopped at three police check-points; each time the police came on to the bus and each time they picked on this man, tipping the contents of his briefcase – a neatly folded clean change of white cotton clothes – on to the floor of the bus, leaving him to pick them up, refold them, and pack them sadly away again until the next search. "Why do they do it?" Megan wanted to know. "It's not fair – he had everything so neat and tidy."

Each time we stopped for police, the bus jolted and jerked while it was stationary; then we stopped again, for no apparent reason, and again were jolted in our seats by a series of sudden jerks. The next time this happened, I got out to investigate, and found that the driver was carefully tightening all the wheel nuts with a huge spanner. For the rest of the journey, this was done once every half hour; presumably, and alarmingly, it was necessary.

The hills, the Siva Lekh, gradually grew steeper as they merged with the Mahabharat foothills, and we were soon climbing steeply and steadily, with one half-hour stop for lunch at a transport café where tea, hot curried beans, spicy pastries, and biscuits were available. The café was on a hairpin bend above the Rapti River. Several men were squatting among the tumbled stones of the bank relieving themselves, and we could not help noticing, and being shocked by, one bared bottom with a severe prolapsed condition which must have been acutely painful and needed urgent medical attention.

For four hours after lunch we stopped only for nut tightening. We were on the Raj Path, Nepal's first long-distance road, an Indian feat of engineering which deserves a place among the wonders of the world. Later roads in Nepal show some improvement in design and technology, but none can boast more hairpin bends to the mile or be more spectacular. The new Raj Path replaced a track of the same name which was previously the only recognizable route to the border south of Kathmandu. All the luxuries acquired abroad by the Ranas – chandeliers, fine furniture, even cars – were brought into the country on the backs of porters along the old Raj Path, which was slightly more direct but even steeper, until one of the Ranas was considerate enough to introduce a rope way which made keeping his family in the Rana style slightly less strenuous.

At times, as we snaked up the side of the Mahabharat Mountains for several thousand feet of bend after tight bend, the turning space on the corners was so confined that the bus could only get round by reversing, edging forwards, reversing again, and then swinging slowly over an alarming drop. Looking down we could often see twenty or more hairpin bends looping below us, the drop from one down to the next almost sheer. Sometimes landslides had half obliterated sections of the road and not yet been completely cleared, so that we were on an angle as we negotiated the bends, and on much of the road there was only space for one bus or lorry at a time, and the only way for two to pass each other was for one to reverse out of the way into a wider passing place. Fortunately, there was little traffic, and on the whole journey we saw no more than half a dozen private cars.

The slope was too steep for even a Nepalese farmer to carve fields out of the mountainside forest. The earliest rhododendrons were splashes of brilliant red among the scrubby dark green bushes and trees whose roots held the hillside in place. From the highest point of the road across the mountains, the view towards Kathmandu was like a delicate Japanese water colour floating away into the distance. A belt of mist obscured the valley and lower slopes of the hills to the north, leaving the mountain peaks suspended from trailing clouds; as daylight softened into evening the pinks and whites of peaks and clouds were unworldly and ethereal and apparently unconnected to the earth's surface.

As we started the descent into the valley, the scenery became gentler, the road more credible. By the time we reached the final police check post, it was dark and we were not far from the valley. The police again came on to the bus, and again I had to produce my passport and repeat my age and date of birth. We had by this time been on the bus for nearly eight hours; I was tired and irritable, and enquired sarcastically whether they would also like to know how many fillings I had in my back teeth. This was unfortunately understood by several of the passengers, and their amusement and my lapse in good humour understandably irritated the police. To my and the children's alarm, I was pulled off the bus to a hut by the road where my passport was checked and re-checked.

Several fellow passengers were being given cholera and TAB jabs at an unhygienic-looking table in front of the police house. I was told to join the queue and roll my sleeve up; otherwise I would not be able to enter the valley. I tried to weigh up the alternatives: would it be better to risk infection from an unnecessary jab, or stay the night at the police station, leaving the children to make their way back to the Waterhouses and hoping David would be able to extricate me next day? It took time, talk, and as much charm as I could muster to persuade the soldier in charge that my papers were all in order, and that we had all had the necesary innoculations in England. When at last I was allowed back on to the bus, I vowed never again to break the unwritten international code of civility, and if necessary servility, to police and officials.

14

The Coronation

Before the coronation, most people in Kathmandu must at some time have been caught in one of the many parades and rehearsals which made even the simplest shopping expedition a matter of guesswork and evasion. During one of the pre-coronation parades, we were at the Singha Durbar, a Rana palace built in the extravagant style of Versailles and now the bureaucratic centre of Nepal. It is approached through an arched gate along a carriageway between gardens and a lake laid out with imperial French formality, but behind its elegant façade a large part of the buildings, and thousands of files and documents, were destroyed by fire some years ago. In the remaining rooms the official business of government is carried out and the paperwork of crazy bureaucracy mounts up.

Wandering off to the right of the palace along a straight narrow drive between high walls and through an open gate, we found ourselves at the back of the military stables. Only a few sick or injured horses had been left in the long covered building divided into roomy loose-boxes, but there were a few young horses loose in the yard, charging round and rearing up at each other. In a sturdy post and rail pen a horse was having its feet smeared with ointment. At one end of the yard, in a large barn-like building, was a collection of old coaches and carriages, most of which had been recently repainted and which had no doubt been carried into the country by porters for the comfort and glory of previous rulers.

While we were looking at the coaches, the parade horses were ridden at a gallop into the yard, clattering and skidding to a halt in a long line. There were about fifty of them, some with plumed browbands, ridden by smartly dressed soldiers. Their captain immediately noticed and challenged us: what were we doing, why were we doing it, who were we, why had we not asked his permission, and why had we come in through the back entrance? We apologized, acknowledged his undoubted authority, expressed our deep and sincere interest in his magnificent horses, and were graciously invited to come again – but through the correct entrance.

As if the parades in preparation for the coronation were not enough, National Democracy Day was celebrated only a few days before the coronation, with an unexciting People's Parade, a homely cheerful procession of Scouts, Guides, womens' institutes and guilds, and schoolgirls in sari uniforms. The *Rising Nepal* reported enthusiastically, reminding its readers that Nepal was a truly democratic and developing country, in case this might otherwise have escaped their attention.

Far more spectacular was a full dress rehearsal about a week before the coronation. A procession of elephants, horses, bands, and foot columns escorted a magnificent coach and horses to the Tundikel, the city's main parade ground, where we were able to walk right up to a row of nineteen elephants standing patiently to attention and draped in gold-painted red silk. Each elephant had a silk-covered box seat strapped to its massive back and was accompanied by an attendant in silk uniform carrying a gilded mounting ladder; behind him another attendant, equally richly dressed, stood discreetly with a bucket and shovel.

On the afternoon before the coronation, we found the elephants in an enclosure behind the Singha Durbar barracks. The keepers, who had been living in tents, were painting ceremonial patterns on trunks, ears, and toe nails, and invited us to go as close as we liked to watch. The elephants squinted at us incuriously through their disproportionately tiny eyes while their giant toenails were painted different bright colours. Then, well behaved and docile, each elephant in turn lowered its bulk to the ground so that its flapping ears could be adorned with multi-coloured flower designs. The painter next climbed on the step made by a bent foreleg to add squirls and more flowers to its huge forehead. Final touches of gold leaf were to be added early on coronation morning.

By evening, there was an atmosphere of excited expectancy, with no sign of the unrest anxiously awaited by officials in high places. Kathmandu seemed to be in a relaxed mood, the people strolling in festive finery in the streets and round the temples. In spite of the erratic nature of the Kathmandu electricity supply, the city gleamed and twinkled after dark. Each temple was festooned with rows of white lights etching the elegant pagoda roofs against the night sky. Shrines were alight with naked bulbs and little wick lamps, and gay with flowers and offerings. Even the terrible god Bhairab, caged behind the grill from which he was allowed to emerge only once a year, was illuminated. The pavilion-like temple on the Tundikel was a mass of delicate fairy lights, and on the other side of the town a lake temple to Shiva set over the water of Rani Pokhari was the most ethereal and beautiful of all, its delicately lighted outline reflected in the surface of the lake, criss-crossed by tinted arches of water from the fountains. Swayambhu shone and shimmered on its hill, floodlit against the dark unlit mountains. The scene was set for rejoicing.

The dawn of coronation day was cold and foggy. The ritual started at 5 a.m., long before we were up. As Nepal has the only remaining Hindu monarchy in the world, it is only in this country that the "ancient vedic rites of anointment and consecration" are still observed. The aim of the complex ceremonies is to enhance the temporal and spiritual qualities of the king, infusing him with a sense of duty to his subjects, and allow him an opportunity to identify with the entire nation – aims no different, it would seem, from those of our own queen's coronation service.

The practice was, however, very different. Before the coronation the king had already had to undergo a variety of rituals to ward off unfortunate incidents or omens and ensure the support of the gods during his reign. For days, the holy scriptures had been chanted almost ceaselessly in the chief temples; the nine planets as well as the innumerable deities had to be appeased and enlisted. The king had been purified by the sprinkling of holy water on his person; ceremonial fires and food-offering had been duly observed. The support of his ancestors had been invoked.

All these details having been attended to in advance, the king and queen arrived in state at the Hanuman Dhoka at 5 a.m., to start the day with a cleansing and anointing ceremony, although the cleansing, with ghee, milk, curd, honey, and water from eight rivers (including of course the sacred Ganges) and the seven seas, was of a spiritual rather than a physical nature. North, south, east and west were represented by members of the different castes, each with a jug containing the relevant anointment. Ghee, from the east, from a gold jug, would bestow vigour; milk from a silver jug, the offering of the south, and curd from a copper jug from the west, were offered by a Kshatriya and a Vaishya respectively: and the honey, from a humble earthenware jug, the offering of the north, would bring glory and popularity. Brahman priests added water sprinkled with holy grass and poured from a golden jug with one hundred spouts, making sure that divine qualities would be bestowed as well as all the human virtues.

Mud from every conceivable source was applied to the different parts of the king's royal body: – from a mountain top, an ant hill, from various powerful animals, from the bottom of a lake, and even from a harlot's door, the ceremony symbolizing his dominance over and concern for every part of his kingdom.

The king in turn prayed to every conceivable item or deity worthy of worship: among them a wick lamp, eight holy mothers, and the nine planets, before sitting on the throne; this was covered with layers of animal skins showing again his power over and interest in even the wild life of his kingdom. All these ceremonies were accompanied by much chanting of holy words, playing of musical instruments, and blowing of conch shells, and at the actual crowning a salvo of guns was fired on the Tundikel. A particularly magnificent royal umbrella held over the king's head and a yak's tail fan ensured his comfort.

The five-hour ceremony was conducted by Brahman priests on an elaborate covered platform specially constructed in the open courtyard of the Hanuman Dhoka, and interrupted half-way for cigarettes and tea. The royal guests, including Prince Charles and Lord Mountbatten from Britain, sat in the front row of specially erected stands. Lord Mountbatten was apparently determined to remember the occasion, and produced an Instamatic camera. David had one of the few passes for western journalists.

For the waiting crowds outside, the end of the religious rituals marked the start of the day's spectacle, as the king rode through the city first on a consecrated stallion, and then on an equally blessed and highly adorned elephant. The main procession, which we had already seen rehearsed, was reserved for the afternoon. The morning mist had cleared; the astrologers had chosen well. The sky was clear and blue, the white tops of the mountains sharp; there was a slight breeze, just enough to counteract the heat of the sun and make the weather comfortably perfect.

Of course, security on the streets was strict, and there were pavements along the royal route on which no one was allowed to linger. But streets and temple steps, and enclosures on the Tundikel for different groups of onlookers, were crowded. Only a line of railings and a policeman separated us from the procession. The Nepalese are experts in the art of colourful pageantry, having plenty of practice in their frequent and spectacular religious ceremonies. Elephants swayed past in majestic splendour, several with waving plumed head-dresses above their red silk skirts and painted flowers, their richly dressed passengers, the women in saris, the men in official costume, rolling slightly on their elevated seats. Behind each elephant, its uniformed bucket and shovel attendant followed anxiously. The king's elephant was, of course, the most magnificent of all, distinguished by elaborate cloth of gold robes. The king himself, although not normally a majestic figure, with owlish glasses and a studious expression, was unmistakably regal in his official robes and gilded pineapple-plumed crown studded with jewels.

Although the elephants were the most exotic and popular part of the long parade, among those on foot the Buddhist monks were the most spectacular and colourful contingent, in brilliant saffron robes and horned masks. Bands, playing eastern and western music, bagpipe regiments, mounted and foot soldiers, were incongruously interspersed with Toyota coaches and cars carrying dignitaries who had not been given elephant space. Other dignitaries, Jaya and Kanti among them, walked in official civil service uniform – white cotton jodhpurs, long white shirts protruding below black jackets, and jaunty sideways peaked black caps for the men, and maroon saris topped inelegantly by long black cardigans for the women.

The crowds were restrained, and smaller than had been expected. The constant rumours about some sort of protest or disturbance had kept many people at home in fear – we later spoke to several people who had not dared to come out, and who afterwards regretted their decision. They could not enjoy the pageantry at home on television, as we can on similar occasions. As the king passed, a subdued ripple of clapping and cheering passed along the pavements and up the pagoda temple steps crowded with women and children in their most brightly coloured clothes. The mood was one of quiet content rather than fervent rejoicing, and there was no untoward incident to mar the day. The procession turned into the Tundikel, the king mounted the throne, and one by one in interminable salutation his subjects and guests paid homage. Civil servants sat on the grass in groups waiting their turn, looking like patient penguins in their black and white.

There are people, even in Nepal, who say that it was the last Hindu coronation the world will ever see; there is no other reigning Hindu monarch and the country has already changed rapidly in the last quarter of a century; further change is inevitable, and in many respects desirable. The king's coronation speeches made this point strongly, but without hinting that change might mean the removal of the monarchy. Some feel that a modified form of Chinese communism would, in the long run, be best for Nepal. Few dare hint that the leadership of the king is less than perfect, but many, although only a minority, say in private that they have been disappointed with the rate of progress in Birendra's early years on the throne, although he is probably the most enlightened and certainly the most widely travelled of any of Nepal's rulers. (He went to schools and colleges in India, England, Japan, and America.) Since the coronation, there has been increasing pressure for changes in the political system in Nepal, particularly from the student population in Kathmandu. Elections have been promised, and concessions made by the king and his government which may mean the end of the present partyless Panchayat system and lessen the power of the monarchy.

The festive mood of coronation day lasted into the evening and for the next few days. After dark, the lights gleamed on temples, flags fluttered across the narrow streets, butter lamps twinkled in shrines. Family parties celebrated at home, in the streets, and at shrines and temples. The ritual of coronation was over, but no Nepalese festivity is ever cut short. The Nepalese Press, of course, gave glowing nationalistic accounts, as is right and proper, and as does our Press on similar occasions.

Once the king had been safely crowned our time in Nepal was nearly over. David had finished filming, and was able to join us with the Waterhouse family on a final picnic trip to Sankhu, a Newari village only a few miles from Kathmandu but rarely visited by tourists as it can only be reached on foot or, as we went, by Land Rover. As a result, it has remained almost entirely unspoilt and medieval; its tall terraced houses, many with intricate carved façades, and wide paved streets, have an air of dilapidated elegance. In the village square, a band was playing as we arrived, and with much banter and laughter they encouraged us to try their instruments. Our efforts were if possible even more cacophonous than theirs.

A gang of boys attached themselves to us, apparently convinced that without their help we would be unable to find the temple of Bajra Jogini above the village or cope with the weight of our picnic basket – which they lightened by surreptitiously sharing a bar of chocolate among themselves. The path led uphill on wide steps, past a single-storey modern health-post building and a shrine and rest shelter where an offering had just been made to a local deity, which looked to us more like a blood-spattered lump of rock. Beside it was a heap of shoes as no one proceeding to the temple was allowed to wear leather for fear of offending the gods. Several holy men were sitting under the shelter in a religious stupor, wearing nothing but loin cloths; their hair was long and matted, a sure sign of sanctity.

Another holy man, a priest, dressed in a long yellow robe and hung about with garlands of marigolds, was intoning prayers on the temple steps as we approached. Although he would not let us look into the Hindu inner sanctuary behind the temple's firmly closed carved doors, he had no objection to posing for photographs. Monkeys jumped on and off animal sculptures on either side of him, and raced round the temple's pagoda roof and paved courtyard, competing for a snatch at our picnic. Jane was about to close her teeth on a sandwich when it was whipped from her hand over her shoulder by a furry paw – the shocked horror on her face was unrepeatable.

When we had eaten, and admired the finely carved wooden and metal panels adorning the main temple and two smaller pagoda-roofed buildings, we climbed more steps to a monastery built round a central courtyard which housed a fine collection of bronzes and a Buddha buried up to his neck. We had timed our visit badly, as we were refused permission to enter for three firm reasons: first, viewing was possible only at 11 a.m., and it was noon; second, the priest had gone to Sankhu, and only he had authority to open the doors (either the priest we had just left had moved fast, or he was the wrong priest);

and third, Buddha was eating and must not be disturbed.

Above the monastery a cave had been cut out of the hillside. A holy place of great antiquity, where a most saintly hermit once withdrew from the world, it is entered through a square stone doorway, with a worn and ancient inscription carved into the lintel, or through a very small window. The legend that only a saint can squeeze through the window implies that all adults are sinners, as it is only big enough for a child. Our children just managed to wriggle their way through.

Saints and sinners alike, we all stood outside the cave for a while, looking down on the gold of the temple roof framed in a gap in dark evergreens. It seemed a suitable place to be on our last day in Nepal: high on a hill below the mountains, above a monastery where Buddha was eating and a Hindu temple where a priest was praying and monkeys prancing over ancient sculpture. As we walked slowly down, the view ahead was of green paddy fields of winter wheat, terraced by patience and hard work from the hillside. Below Sankhu, with its tightly knit community of elegant old houses, the land was a flat for a while; a dry-stone wall, like the walls on Dartmoor, wound along the side of a stony path and round the base of a sudden hill shaped like a pyramid and terraced to the top. On the way back to Kathmandu we stopped at a small isolated brick and tile field where several members of one family were at work.

Our last evening was spent at the Giris', with Jaya and Kanti and Jaya's brother Tulsi, who was then prime minister. We talked until the early hours of the morning, discussing Nepal's past and future, the differences and similarities between British and Nepalese customs and beliefs, and the meanings and problems of kingship and democracy.

Tulsi Giri was largely responsible for drawing up the constitution, but we found it difficult to agree that the monarchy was, as he claimed, constitutional rather than, as David insisted, absolute, and eventually decided that the best description would probably be either "absolute constitutional monarchy" or "constitutional absolute monarchy". We agreed that great progress had been made under Mahendra, and hoped that this would continue under Birendra, accepting Tulsi's optimistic point that as Nepalese development only started in the middle of this century, Nepal had an advantage over other countries and could learn from their mistakes, selecting only the best features of western democracies; but we were still doubtful about whether Nepal should be called a democracy at all.

The discussion was unexpectedly continued next morning at the airport with Mr Pande from the royal palace, who wanted to make sure there was no confusion about the nature of the monarchy by giving David a copy of the constitution. I could not help feeling that the question had little relevance for the majority of the people of Nepal, whose life has changed so little over the centuries.

As we took off, we could see the valley below us with its temples and the uneven lines of the paddy fields climbing the hills, and in the distance the white peaks of the mountains; then the plane began its steep banking turn over the mountains separating the valley from the plains, and Nepal was lost in cloud.

Diary of Megan Lomax, aged Five

First Trek

14th Jan.	We went to see the animals' heads be chopped off.
15th	I saw a baby goat and it nearly bit my trousers.
16th	We walked and we walked up a mountain and I had to keep stopping. I was tired.
18th	We were walking and my ankle started hurting.
19th	We went across a bridge made out of logs. I nearly crawled across it.
20th	We saw some eagles and some flew over us (Gandrung).
21st	We went to a waterfall and we were climbing through the trees. It was very difficult and dangerous.
22nd	We were climbing up a hill and a cloud came down so we could not see properly and it started raining.
23rd	We saw some donkeys and ponies. They had bells round their necks and sacks on their backs.
24th	We saw a pony in the river and it was dead because it had a broken neck.
25th	We went up the hill and we played in the snow. When we came back we had to take our clothes off to dry them over the fire (Gorepani).
26th	When we were walking along we saw a baby monkey and it jumped on to Alistair's shoulder and bit his parka.
27th	We are staying at the British farm school. They have rabbits to sell to the people for food and they have lights and loos and a shower.

28th	We were walking barefoot and I kept running and jumping.
29th	We walked to Pokhara and I bought some sweets and a bag.
31st	Yesterday we went on a bumpy bus. Today we went in a big canoe on the lake. There was an earthquake.

Megan's Second Trek

1st day	We went across some stones on some rivers and I was holding Mummy's hand some of the time. She nearly fell in and nearly pulled me in with her.
2nd day	Tonight we are going to sleep outside on a balcony.
3rd day	We went to the Tibetan new year and had a tika. That is lumps on our heads of fat.

David or I helped with the more difficult spellings but Megan chose all the words. After this, Megan gave up the effort of writing in her diary, and instead drew pictures to illustrate what we did.

Alistair's diary was a pretty scrappy effort, but he took some excellent photographs, from which he later made his own prints.

Extracts from Jane Lomax's Diary (aged Eleven)

First day in Kathmandu: We walked down the street and came on to the market. Immediately we were surrounded by people trying to make us buy post cards, stamps, pendants, pipes, models of Buddha etc.

We walked round the little tiny streets and looked at the houses. I could not stand the smell – how anyone lives there, I don't know.

Went to see Kanti, and the room was very, very, cold.

Visit to Dakshin Khali temple: we got a taxi and went sixteen miles from the town, winding along roads that cling to the hillside. On the way to the temple, we saw a wild cat. At the temple, we saw a man sprinkling a goat with water. He then untied it, grabbed its head and started to saw its head off. Its head hanging off, the goat still appeared to be moving. It was the most horrible thing I have seen in my life.

At the Giris': Kanti had just been decorated, for being the Queen's doctor, and she had delivered all the queen's babies. It was the second time she had had a medal. The medal had a kukri in the centre, and that is the sign of bravery.

The nights get very cold, very quick.

First Trek

First day: note: while trekking, distance is not measured in miles but in hours.

Sherpas (the porters) are fantastically strong and have massive calf muscles. Megan is the youngest trekker ever to have walked along this path.

On the way we saw someone grind rice.

Second trekking day: We started at 8 o'clock. The first part was easy, walking along the track, through a village. We then came out on to some paddy fields and walked along them, through the valley, until we came to a large hill. Then, wow! we went up and up and although it was not all that steep it was a long way as the steps wiggled about. When we reached the top (about two hours, nearly 1,000 feet, counting stops) it was a fairly easy walk along a ledge. We then continued to walk through different villages, along what, in the monsoon, become rivers, gushing down the mountain side.

We saw plenty of animals, including eagles, sheep, goats, and buffaloes.

It was the farthest I have ever walked in my life, and it took eight hours, including stops, and we went up 2,000 feet. It was about ten miles. The scenery all the way has been fantastic, with the rivers in the valley, and the terraces, that have been dug by hand, down on all sides, and covered in winter wheat and rice. We are staying in a handwoven shelter-house, about 12 by 6 feet.

Third day trekking: I woke up at about 6.30 and went outside, leaving the porters snoring like mad. Dad was taking some pictures of the mountains, and I arrived just in time to see them go pink as the sun touched the peaks. We then went inside and had some tea and an omelette each. When we had eaten, we asked when Sonam and the porters would eat. They replied: "We will not eat, there is nothing to eat." We felt very guilty then.

The people here are just fighting to get into the army, preferably the British army, as they get a pension.

All the time, we are seeing sweetcorn hanging or built in a wall on stakes off the ground to be dried by the sun. While I wrote this, about twenty children appeared and watched and some women came and made relevant gestures to Mum, asking if we were her children!

Nearly everyone smokes, including the children, and the adults make the children come up to you and ask for cigarettes. While we were walking, we had to stop every so often for Megan to catch up. Although she was walking, she was a bit slow, and a *little* bit tired.

Just before supper, we played with some of the village children, making hoops out of bamboo.

At Gandrung: we went up to the school, and were immediately surrounded by children. Dad took some pictures of the schoolchildren and the village behind. We stood on a hill and watched some eagles. They came fantastically close and Dad had his camera out in a minute (telephoto lens) and all the children started shrieking, and one threw a stone. I didn't understand but I think he was told off. The eagle came within ten feet of Alistair. It had an eight-foot wing span and its tail and wing tip feathers were turned up to catch the thermal current.

Leaving Gandrung: breakfast was the best meal I had had for ages, not having rice – at least, it had rice, but in a lovely porridge, and then we had an omelette each.

Then we went up and up. The only nice thing about that was that we saw seven eagles at once.

Later we saw a lot more eagles, and some ex-Gurkhas building a wall, like the ones you see on Dartmoor.

Cchomrung: the Sara falls expedition: it was very difficult, but we found the falls in the end. After washing in the ice-cold water (I will not say what Alistair did!) we moved on. After five minutes we were clinging to a rock face and holding on to bamboos, tree roots, and branches. After Solti had managed to climb a tree, we managed to get down. There was no path. I was not frightened, for I have always wanted to do some mountaineering, but the amount of things that broke beneath Dad's weight was alarming.

Tirkhe Dunge: on the way, the mountains were covered with cloud, and only at times could you see the peaks, and only a small bit of them. Dad suddenly thought of a name for a book, if one of us writes one: *A Walk through the Clouds*.

When we reached Tirkhe Dunge, a long train of donkeys came past, then in a few minutes another train came in the opposite direction. Both had ponies as well, and ponies and donkeys were very heavily laden and looked very hungry. After they had gone by, a tiny little puppy came up and tugged at Alistair's shoe lace. Alistair tried to get his foot away. Then followed a tug of war. In the night, I was kept awake quite a bit by rats who yelled, squeaked and scratched all night. Dad said he had not slept at all, but Mummy said when she was awake he had been asleep.

In the forest: we walked through a large forest of rhododendrons, and saw a lot of mules carrying salt, potatoes, and milk powder. One man spoke very good English and Dad started talking to him for about $\frac{3}{4}$ hour. While he was talking we heard a crash, but didn't take much notice. We walked on and then at the bridge saw what the crash had been.

A man was sitting down near the water, with a pony's head in his hands, prodding at its eyes. Another man was taking off the pack from its back. The pony was lying in a twisted position, and had obviously fallen off the bridge. Sonam came climbing down just as another man appeared, who started to yell at the man getting the pack off the pony's back. Dad said he was saying, "You stupid fool! You should have been there to guide him away from the edge."

Sonam shouted, and then he called to us, "He's dead, I think." This was confirmed when the halter was taken off and the head let go so that it fell back into the stream. I have never seen a dead pony before, and I don't want to again.

Gorepani: when we reached Gorepani, we were happily surprised at what we found to sleep in. It had a menu. Here is what we had for dinner: tomato soup, omelette, fried bread and peanut butter, chapatti and honey. What a meal!

Just before we went to bed, Sonam and Solti appeared, obviously whacked. They had had three glasses of raxi each, and it's powerful stuff.

The porters went to a party with two didi (women) and did not appear till next day, looking very sheepish.

After climbing Poonhill: some hippies came in and walked around, not bothering to say hello. Once in they started to smoke pot – they smoke around 10 grams a day. I didn't like them, especially when they started ordering the manager around. Dad and Mum always tell us to be polite to people and not take them for granted. One obviously came from a very rich family, with servants. Mum asked one what he did for a living. He replied, "Anything I want."

I was not very well in the night. Mum said it was the altitude. I had a tummy ache and felt sick and had a head ache.

Birethanti: we are staying in the nicest place yet, with lovely food. It was a lovely sight when a mule train came over the suspension bridge, stepping very carefully as it rocked up and down. I was nearly pushed into the river, which is very fast.

Visit to the Khamba camp from Pokhara: by 9 o'clock, we were on the bus to the Indian border – we weren't going that far, only about twenty miles. We had gone for twenty minutes when the bumps and tea began to have effect. Dad asked the driver if we could get out for a few minutes – what a fool I felt, squatting by the bus!

After climbing up, and up, and up, and up, and then up some more, we came to a place full of police and military people. The head man spoke English and Dad and he talked for some time. Then Dad asked if we could look round. He (the headman) was obviously upset, but agreed in the end, providing no photos were taken. As soon as we got into the camp, lots of people came round, fantastic faces and clothes. They were living in houses or the majority in tents. These were very small indeed and they lived in them all year round. There was a long row of tents and one very long hut made of mats. This must have had about 150 people living in it. There was a lama's tent with holy designs on it.

When Dad started to ask questions, the sneaky little man nearly burst a blood vessel and got us out of the camp.

Phewa dam: we went to see the DAM THAT WAS. When we got there, it was an amazing sight. Half of it had collapsed. It was still lying in great pieces on the river bed that was. Nobody had bothered to move them. The story of the dam is this: fifteen years ago (when Dad was first in Nepal), an Indian building company was building it. The engineers had sold the cement, and after making a huge profit built the dam with rotten cement. Six weeks ago, the Nepalese repaired it. Three weeks later the dam broke, very embarrassing.

Earthquake: we were sitting in the hotel when the whole building began to shake. Everyone in the hotel looked up and Dad said it was the generator. Then, as the whole structure shook again, he rushed to the window. It was shaking violently now, and my one thought was to get out before it fell down. Once outside it stopped, and I looked up to see Mum and Dad on the balcony. "Come up," they shouted. I shook my head and backed into the road, but a few minutes later I consented. The manager explained: "It's a violent earth tremor, the worst we have had." He had been on the roof when it started and one of the waiters had been carrying some tea and dropped it. We were laughing about it now and talking about earthquakes, for that's what it was.

Soon after we went to bed and in the night I woke up to find myself in the worst thunderstorm I have ever been in. I went to sleep feeling very wronged: where had the wonderful Nepalese weather gone to? I wanted to get out of Pokhara, before the town collapsed.

Some comments in the Kathmandu valley:

Now we are back in Kathmandu, we have to do school work set at home. School now seems (as does England) far away and very unreal, as if it was never really there, and this is the only life I have known.

National Democracy Day: Mummy and I went out to see the parade in Kathmandu to celebrate this wonderful occasion, although maybe it would be rather drab. It was. Rows and rows of people chatting passed us, and the pavement was thick with people.

Coronation procession rehearsal: David Waterhouse rang up to say there was a full-scale rehearsal of the coronation parade going on in the town. We left our school work and got a taxi to the nearest point we could, as the roads had been blocked. We got to the Annapurna hotel when we heard some music, and saw the start of the procession. There were different kinds of bands, playing Western and Indian and Nepalese music, all at once, and different kinds of soldiers, mainly Gurkhas. When they went, some horses and flag bearers came past, and then they all stopped, turned, and went back. We went through the hotel and saw the same thing all over again. After that we were swallowed up in the main flow of the crowd and found ourselves at the edge of the road up which more people were coming. But after them came some more horses and a number of rather boring posh cars, with important-looking people in them. Three policemen had tried to move us, but Mum pointed at Megan and said she was too small and would not see. They probably did not understand, but they let us stay.

Then came one of the best bits. Six bay horses (very like Twiggy, my pony, but thicker set) harnessed to a magnificent newly painted carriage that the king will ride in on the day.

The procession passed and everybody started to move. I hated the crowd of people and felt like thumping and hitting my way out, so that I could breathe some fresh air. We walked to the gate of the parade ground and waited there for about ten minutes until we saw something happening further up. The police made us go the right way round a temple/roundabout, but then did nothing to stop us going into the parade ground, where the procession had come and had scattered and sat down in groups.

What most people were looking at were four ornately decorated elephants; then, just as we arrived, so did fifteen more. They were dressed in red silk or satin, that flowed when they moved, with velvet-covered seats on top. One had fantastic tusks, but the others had had theirs removed. Megan was terrified!

Second Trek

First day: today we woke up at 6.45, and had a two-hour bus journey to where we would start our second trek. We walked for five hours. Alistair had cramp in his leg, and it would not hold his colossal weight. Megan had about ten different loose teeth, and asked questions like "How deep is the sea?" and I had tummy ache.

At Bonapati, where we would sleep, there was a little dog, and he started eating my sleeping bag.

Second day: today we had no breakfast until the next village, where we had two fried eggs and some beans. This was our lunch as well. Then followed a big climb, but on the way we bought some bananas – it is not the time when they are best, but they were delicious.

When we reached Dubachour, we found we had done what we had thought would take seven hours in four! So we decided to go on to Kakani. This took about three hours, but then we walked on to the next village quite a bit higher. We reached it at 4 o'clock. There was no hotel or guest house, so we asked at some houses if we could stay. All refused, and we were going to go on to Sermatang. We did not want to, as we would not reach it until about 8 o'clock. Then, at the last house, we were allowed to stay. We had to sleep on the balcony as the house was small and there was already a family of five sleeping in the one room. We had a much nicer supper, rice and vegetables. These people (lamas) don't each much dahl. Then Mummy asked for some tato raxi (hot rakshi) and Alistair and I were given some. I slept well! Then we went to bed, and I dreamt of a never-ending road, going up!

Third day: Tarke Ghyang: we are staying in a lama's house, and it is very nice and clean. All the pots are shiny and are arranged round the shelves.

We went out to explore, and after fifteen minutes came across a courtyard filled with people chanting and eating. We were beckoned inside and offered some revolting rice chapattis. Then we had a tika – that is, we went up to the lama and had some flour mixed with sugar and had three lumps of fat on our hair. The fat made our hair all sticky and horrible.

After supper, we went back to the courtyard, to find people singing and dancing, and much raxi was being consumed. We were pulled into the circle of dancing, singing people and Alistair and I had to dance.

Fourth day: we had a cup of tea before leaving for Timbu, about six hours' downhill walk. After two hours, we reached another Kakani, where we had breakfast – vegetable, fried chapattis, double omelette, and tea. Then it took only $2\frac{1}{2}$ hours to reach Timbu, so KV said why not go on to Chiul. We walked around some more hills in a sweltering 80 degrees with no breeze. Twice we sat down under a tree and would have sat down more times if there had been any more trees or shade of any sort.

When we reached Chiul, it was a tiny place. After a bit of discussion we decided we had better stay here at the Helambu Hotel – it called itself a hotel, but how we shall all fit in I don't know. (We did.)

Fifth day: as usual we did not have breakfast where we stayed. We were walking along the path above the river as the people we stayed with told KV lots of stories about robbers and bandits on the river. KV refused to go that way.

Sixth day: on the way we were walking along a ridge and had a fantastic view down either side, into two valleys.

The house we stayed in was very large and had a big balcony being built around the house, by one man. From here we could see the

Kathmandu valley for the first time in a week. It was nice, but not so nice, if you see what I mean.

Seventh day: we walked for about twenty minutes to the hydro-electric dam. It was smaller than the dam in Pokhara and it worked! About ten minutes later we were on an unmade road and walked along this until we reached the place we had breakfast. Nearby there was a fantastic Hindu temple, and Mummy and Megan walked round it, and saw people having tikas (paint on their foreheads) as it was the first official day of spring. Then we walked along the flat, and I think boring, road to Bodnath. This is a large stupa with shops surrounding it. The stupa is said to contain a relic of the Buddha, maybe an eyelash or a toenail.

The Terai

This is a flat part of Nepal, and until not long ago only few people could live here other than the Terai people because of malaria. There is still malaria there now. We flew to Simra. Simra is only 450 feet above sea level – our own house in England is 600 feet. We were amazed by the way the hills stopped and the Terai started. One minute we were in the mountains – well, hills, but they are about 9,000 feet – and the next it was flat jungle and farmland. When the plane landed, it was a perfect landing, the best so far. We walked through the aerodrome and on to a bus to go to Birganj about five kilometres from the Indian border.

The road was perfectly straight and on either side we could see farmland not unlike some in England. There were some trees and pylons stretching as far as the eye could see. We saw lots of oxen pulling ploughs and carts. They were the traditional oxen with large hump-withers.

When we arrived at Birganj we wandered around a bit and then went into an office for tourist information. The man there said the Hotel Rapti was a good place for lunch. It was a bit grotty, but we're used to it by now.

After lunch we got into two rickshaws and had a tour of the town. It was not a very interesting town but we enjoyed it.

No plane seats, no plane – we will have to go back by bus.

The bus journey: we went to the Terai to see a different part of Nepal. I was very cross when it got dark on the way back and we could not see out, on the journey to Hetauda. At the bus station they had said it would take an hour and a half, but after leaving at five we arrived at 8.30. This included five police checks though.

I will not say much about the journey from Hetauda to Kathmandu, except that it was some of the most beautiful scenery I have ever seen. The road was so twisty; the most hairpin bends we did at one time was twelve! Travelling on a Nepalese or Indian bus is something not far removed from packing sardines in a tin and then playing hockey with the tin as a ball. At least that's what it felt like, and our trip was luxury compared with some of them.

There were too many police checks to count. One man from India had all his things in his case neatly folded and the police scrumped them up. Mummy even had to put her age on a form. We arrived in Kathmandu at 8 p.m. and my tooth came out.

Coronation Day

It was nasty to see all the police had fixed bayonets. We went to the parade ground at 2 o'clock. It was not until 3.30 that we saw any sign of the procession, but it was well worth it. First came some army bands and soldiers. All the bands were playing Westernish music and one even the Durham Reel, and all at once. The only band not playing Western music had flutes (Nepali kind), drums, and cymbals. This was rather good, with fantastic costumes. Then there were soldiers in kilts playing the bagpipes.

Then came the horses. They were all thoroughbred types and walked in time to the music. They were ridden by the horse guards of Nepal, I suppose, and followed by the elephants. The elephants were what people had been waiting for. They were dressed in the long silk robes like when we saw them at the practice. They had seats on which sat Ranas and people in high position, also some ambassadors, the Russian for one. In the midst of all these robed and painted elephants came a huge elephant, with enormous tusks. It had a gold robe and was painted gold as well as the yellow, red, green, blue, and brown of the other elephants. On its back was the most magnificent chair thing. It had gold on it and a royal (for of course it was the king's) parasol.

And in it sat King Birendra and the Queen. He had been crowned between 5 and 10 a.m. and was wearing the crown. It has a lovely plume of bird of paradise feathers on it. As he passed nobody cheered; there were just polite namastes and clapping. The king looked rather like Mr Kennedy, my housemaster, only Mr Kennedy has ginger hair! When the king had gone by, more elephants came, and then more horses and more people. In the middle of the horses and people came a row of official-looking cars with (I suppose) royalty from other countries reclining on the back seats.